A PERSONAL SUCCESS TOOL KIT

10 Proven Success Boosting Tools to Ignite Your Mental Energy, Enrich Creativity, Enhance Motivation, and Increase Productivity!

By
Robert D. Hutchings

Top Life Books
info@toplifebooks.com
USA

COPYRIGHTS

A PERSONAL SUCCESS TOOL KIT: 10 Proven Success Boosting Tools to Ignite Your Mental Energy, Enrich Creativity, Enhance Motivation, and Increase Productivity!

Robert D. Hutchings Author

AlL Rights Reserved. No part of this publication may be reproduced, distributed, or transmitted in any form or by any means, including photocopying, recording, or other electronic or mechanical methods, without prior written permission from the author, except in the case of brief quotations embodied in critical reviews and certain other non-commercial uses permitted by copyright law. First Printing: December 2025.

Copyright@2025 Robert D. Hutchings

ISBN: 979-8-9874008-2-1
Top Life Books   Top Publishing LLC
info@toplifebooks.com

ACKNOWLEDGEMENTS

I wish to thank and acknowledge my wonderful wife for her invaluable encouragement, help, and support—without which this book would still be just an idea.

Why Read This Book

A PERSONAL SUCCESS TOOL KIT: 10 Proven Success Boosting Tools to Ignite Your Mental Energy, Enrich Creativity, Enhance Motivation, and Increase Productivity!

In this book, I share ten proven, effective techniques successful people use every day. I describe each powerful tool and how each one will help you achieve more productive results in your life. I share the features and benefits of each tool (personal success technique) to help you better understand how they will bless your life. Finally, I give you simple directions on how to use each proven technique to expand your your personal prosperity or entrepreneurial success.

- Do you have the confidence in yourself to manage obstacles and challenges to achieve your goals?

- Can you imagine, visualize, or see yourself realizing every dream of success in your life? If so, this book is for you!

About the Author
Robert D. Hutchings

Robert D. Hutchings is the author of self-help books. He is a board certified clinical hypnotherapist, audiobook narrator, and US Army veteran. Robert completed post-graduate programs in Broadcast Announcing through KBW at UCLA and Advanced Hypnotherapy through HMI. Business Management and Marketing are his undergraduate foundation. Robert worked in radio station management for 15 years. Changing career paths, he entered the year-long Advanced Hypnotherapy program at HMI. After graduation, Robert became board certified as a Clinical Hypnotherapist through the ICBCH and opened his own private hypnosis practice. Since 2011, Robert has successfully helped people fix issues such as poor self-confidence, self-defeating behaviors, stress, anxiety, and more than 350 others. As the author of self-help books, Robert is drawing upon his training, real-life experience, and passion for helping others live more abundant and successful lives.

Preface

I wish I could say this book is totally my own creation. However, I must admit that much of this book came via divine guidance. I opened my laptop and began writing one day. As I wrote, the ideas came pouring on to the page as if they had only been waiting for me to begin. I tell you this so you might understand that despite my flaws as a writer, the content you are about to read is scientifically proven to be effective.

Since this book is the collaboration between man and the divine, you are indeed being given truth. This book is not full of fluff like so many other "self-help" books deliver. This book is the truth. This book offers you real tools. The kind of tools that are solid, powerful, and from which success is born.

The key to success is effort. Do not allow this book to sit on the shelf gathering dust. Put it next to your bed with paper and pen. Write down your thoughts and ideas. Then go to work making great things happen in your life! I wish you happiness and success in your quest to achieve magnificent goals.

Contents

1. THE SCIENCE OF MENTAL CURRENCY   1
2. MENTAL ENERGY & SUCCESS   9
3. GOAL SETTING   18
4. TIME MANAGEMENT METHODS   30
5. VISUALIZATION   47
6. POSITIVE AFFIRMATIONS   58
7. CBT & MINDFULNESS MEDITATION   71
8. SELF-HYPNOSIS FOR SUCCESS   87
9. SPIRITUALITY   101
10. RELATIONSHIPS   116
11. LEARNING   129
12. UNPACKING YOUR SUCCESS TOOLS   138

Endnotes   148

Chapter One

THE SCIENCE OF MENTAL CURRENCY

Introduction to Mental Currency

Dr. Wayne Dyer, a noted self-help author and motivational speaker, is credited with saying, *"Your thoughts are the mental currency that attract success!"* Dr. Dyer wrote several books illuminating positive thinking and the law of attraction. His was the view that our thoughts can literally bring about reality; that changing your thoughts will change your life; and that your success in life depends upon your thoughts and ideas—your **mental currency.**

Albert M. Greenfield, a multimillionaire real estate developer, once noted that **"A man doesn't need brilliance, he only needs mental energy."** His meaning is clear. The value of a man or woman's **mental energy** outweighs the value of the person's intellect when it comes to achieving success. In other words, he is saying, **"Success only requires mental currency."**

Not much has been written about mental currency. It is not a term you hear in financial circles. When I speak about mental currency, I am referring to your thoughts, ideas, creativity, and the power of the mind. Because the **true value** of your **mental currency** is measured by your level of **mental energy**, I share multiple ways to increase your **mental energy** levels throughout this book.

Your mental energy level is directly interrelated to your level of success. Here is a comparison:

High mental energy levels: Your brain is humming with exciting new ideas, thoughts, and goals. You have mental clarity, enthusiasm, and creativity. You move from task to task throughout the day to achieve dreams and goals. Your mental currency, like the price of gold, is increasingly more valuable.

Low mental energy levels: Your brain power is drained. You have little or no creativity, feel foggy-minded, lack enthusiasm, procrastinate, and never set any goals. Additionally, low mental energy makes every task seem heavier, and you end up relying on caffeine to get through the day. Your mental currency, like an ounce of beach sand, has decreasing value.

The purpose of this book, **A Personal Success Tool Kit,** is to provide you with ten proven personal success boosting tools to ignite mental energy, enrich creativity, enhance motivation, and increase productivity! In short, this book will **boost the value of your mental currency!**

Whether you are an entrepreneur dealing with the daily challenges of a business or on a personal quest to "grasp the brass ring," keep this book close because it contains the tools and techniques used by millions of successful individuals over centuries of time. You will transform your life to one of **purposeful personal success** through the power of **increased mental energy.**

The Science Behind Mental Energy

Mental energy is crucial to your ability to execute daily cognitive functions. It is your **power to perform cognitive tasks** like thinking, problem solving, concentrating, memory, and well-being. According to neuroscience, our mental energy impacts three primary spectrums: cognition, feelings of energy or fatigue, and motivation.

The *amygdala, hippocampus,* and *prefrontal cortex* are crucial to the brain's ability to regulate emotions, cognitive control, and memory. Chronic stress can negatively impact the amygdala, hippocampus, and prefrontal cortex's individual function. It can also shrink the size of the hippocampus, leading to problematic learning, emotional dysregulation, and memory difficulties.

Mitochondria produce the energy our brain cells require in order to function. These finite powerhouses act to shape mental health and influence how we feel, think, and ultimately experience the world. Mitochondria can be stimulated externally to either increase or decrease energy conversion through our positive or negative social experiences.

Our brain requires high levels of energy. It consumes 20 percent of our body's total energy supply and relies primarily on just two sources of energy: *glucose*, which is the sugar produced from foods, and *Ketones*, which are produced as the body burns fat. Mitochondria turn these two fuels into energy. It's important to understand that if the brain lacks sufficient energy to function as it should, mental health can be affected.

The neurotransmitters controlling our mental energy include *dopamine, serotonin, orexin, norepinephrine, histamine, acetylcholine, adenosine,* and *glutamate*. Each plays a role in processing and using mental energy. Since dopamine and serotonin are most often identified with mental energy, we will consider these in more detail.

Dopamine, the feel-good chemical messenger, is associated with feeling pleasure, happiness, a positive mood, and feelings of satisfaction. Dopamine is also called the "motivation molecule" because it drives goal achievement and taking on new challenges.

Meditation, listening to music, and completing difficult tasks boost our dopamine levels while elevating mental energy.

Serotonin functions differently from dopamine. Its purpose is to assist in controlling anxiety and emotional health. Engaging in physical exercise, enjoyable relationships, and uplifting social connections boosts serotonin levels while reducing anxiety, increasing feelings of well-being, and revitalizing our mental energy.

Your mental energy level matters. Memory, recall, thinking, concentrating, intricate problem-solving, and mental well-being are all dependent upon mental energy. Your motivation, mood, and ability to cope with the daily stressors and setbacks are also impacted by your level of mental energy. Sustaining a healthy cognitive response to everyday situations is contingent upon the quality of your mental energy.

Brain Energy Theory & Energy Deficits

The brain energy theory suggests that mental illnesses are the result of a malfunction within the brain's energy production mechanism. It considers how the metabolism, mitochondria, and brain perform during energy production rather than focusing only on potential neurotransmitter imbalances.

Simply put, balanced cognitive energy is critical for good mental health and overall wellness. Many mental health disorders have one thing in common: difficulties with the brain's energy metabolism. Research suggests that *depression, schizophrenia,* and *bipolar disorder* are linked to poor energy use, mitochondrial dysfunction, and inflammation.

The following are a few mental health disorders caused by mental energy deficits:

- **Depression:** Production of low brain energy may be associated with sluggish brain activity, low motivation, and relentless sadness.

- **Schizophrenia:** Deficits of energy in key areas of the brain may blight perception and cognitive function.

- **Bipolar Disorder:** Severe mood swings may be connected to energy level fluctuations in the brain.

- **Anxiety Disorders:** An overexcited stress response can deplete energy reserves in the brain and bring on unwarranted fear and worry.

Neuroscientists have come to understand health factors that disrupt energy production, lead to energy deficiencies, and potentially affect mental health.

The following are some of the most common factors that drain mental energy. You might want to evaluate your lifestyle to discover if any of these problem areas are negatively affecting your mental energy levels.

- **Chronic Stress:** Increased cortisol levels caused by stress can cause damage to your mitochondria, resulting in damage to energy metabolism.

- **Poor Sleep Habits:** Sufficient sleep is critical for the repair of mitochondria and the elimination of waste in your brain.

- **Poor Diet:** A diet high in sugar and processed foods causes insulin resistance, inflammation in your body, and reduces brain energy levels.

- **Exposure to Toxins:** Pesticides, poisons, heavy metals, and other environmental toxins impair the function of your mitochondria.

- **Overwork:** Heavy workloads, multitasking, and work-related deadlines all demand mental energy, yet can drain mental energy.

- **Lack of Activity:** No exercise, sitting all day, and letting the body pile on weight, drains mental energy and leads to poor mental or physical health.

- **Unhealthy Habits:** Avoid substance abuse, highly caffeinated energy drinks, unnecessary medications, and high-fat/deep-fried foods.
- **Heredity:** The genetic factor means some are predisposed to the dysfunction of their mitochondria.
- **Lack of Variety:** Boredom leads to lower mental energy. Avoid repetitive tasks, boring routines, and a lack of creative or energizing input.

Now that you have a better understanding of mental energy, why it matters, and the factors that affect it, let's examine methods for protecting and strengthening mental energy. In the following chapters, you'll find proven, helpful methods to assist you in protecting and increasing your mental energy.

Chapter Two

MENTAL ENERGY & SUCCESS
How to Protect Mental Energy

Our brain's ability to perform cognitive tasks such as thinking, decision-making, concentrating, problem-solving, memory, and learning is truly an amazing and indispensable God-given gift. All we have to do is manage the mental energy that makes it all work, and we are good to go. However, the cognitive energy required to wield this gift is often misunderstood or, worse, taken for granted.

Through the process of **energy homeostasis**, balancing energy intake and expenditure is managed subconsciously by the *hypothalamus*, which means we are totally unaware of the status of our mental energy until it is needed. In addition, our mental energy level is unpredictable because it fluctuates throughout the day.

The point is that we must **either react** to problematic challenges when mental energy levels are low or **become proactive** to protect our mental energy in order to maintain consistent levels of mental energy. The most suitable answer to this dilemma is to be *proactive and protect mental energy* in order to maintain cognitive energy and function on demand.

The following is a list of several **proactive mental energy defense strategies** shown by research to protect mental energy levels from dropping too low due to daily stressors.

Prioritize Self-Care: Pay attention to every physical need of your body. Especially drink enough water to stay hydrated so your brain doesn't dry out like an old sponge. Dehydration can have lasting effects on mental energy.

Manage Stress: Be aware of the stress which you place on your body. Anything that stresses your body will reduce your cognitive energy. You may have to lighten your load and learn to say "No" when asked to take on more.

Regular Exercise: Activity increases oxygen flow to your brain, increases serotonin, and reduces brain fog. You benefit from improved stamina, mental energy, and feelings of well-being.

Healthy Diet: Eliminate processed foods, reduce sugar intake, and consume low-fat, whole foods. Reduce caffeine and limit alcohol. Consume nutritious foods to boost mood, enhance physical energy, and maintain mental energy.

Take Breaks: Recharge with short breaks during periods of hard work or activity. Engage in enjoyable activities to break up stressful situations. You might use an alarm to signal regular break periods. Rest and refresh during each break period.

Change Scenery: Working in a different area can provide you with a mental boost. Try changing to a different workstation or desk for a day. Work at a coffee shop or library. If your workplace is noisy, try a quiet place to boost mental energy.

Brain-Boosting Activities: Involve yourself in new activities, take community classes, or write in a journal. Take up new hobbies such as gardening, oil painting, or cooking. Staying mentally active keeps your mental energy revved up.

Take a Nap: A thirty-minute nap during the day boosts physical and mental energy. Find a comfortable chair or couch, or lie on the floor. Totally relax your body and mind to re-energize. Naps help hearts, lower blood pressure, and increase cognitive energy.

Read a Book: As simple as it sounds, reading a novel or nonfiction book is a great way to leave a stress-laden world behind. As we employ our theater of the mind to visualize stories or information, we unleash additional cognitive energy resources.

Friends and Family: Spending time with good friends or with family can help to protect mental energy. Take time to enjoy social and personal relationships. It can engage your brain-boosting neurotransmitters to improve mood and relaxation.

Studies show these strategies to be very helpful for protecting and maintaining mental energy levels in top condition. These protective strategies will also increase your mental energy level.

Building a mindset that is resilient is foundational for anyone on the road to success. Fostering resilience also includes physical vitality because you need a healthy body in order to have a healthy, sharp mind.

10 Ways to Increase Mental Energy

In this section, you will be introduced to ten science-backed methods for increasing your mental energy. Each method is a proven, safe, and effective success tool that works in combination with other strategies as well as stands on its own to heighten your personal success. Each method will be expanded in the following chapters.

1. Goal Setting: When you break big goals into smaller chunks or steps, you gain a sense of progress—a feeling of being in control of your life and accomplishments. This sense of progress activates your brain's reward process to release the feel-good neurotransmitters, which generate the neuro reaction of motivation and pleasure. These feel-good chemicals, coupled with your sense of progress, will increase mental energy levels to maximum levels.

2. **Time Management:** Time management substantially increases mental energy by adding to your sense of being in control. As you implement clear plans, organize project tasks into smaller segments, and set realistic deadlines, you eliminate feelings of overwhelm, anxiety, and stress. Good time management includes accommodating work-life balance, maintaining mental health, and avoiding burnout.

3. **Visualization:** Visualization or mental imagery is associated with increased mental energy through key physiological and psychological means. Visualization stimulates neural pathways in the same manner as if you were actually experiencing the event being visualized, and it also helps to improve overall cognitive health in several different ways. When you visualize your achievements prior to taking action, you conserve mental energy that may otherwise be spent navigating the real, yet unfamiliar, challenge.

4. Positive Affirmations: Positive affirmations tap into the power of subconscious behavior to gently shift your focus so as to improve positive behavior and thinking. When you write down behavior you wish to incorporate into your life and phrase it using present-tense-active verbiage, you create a powerful tool for developing cognitive clarity, better decision-making, trust, reduced mental fog—the list is unlimited. Positive affirmations are like having a wild card for increasing your mental energy.

5. Cognitive Behavioral Therapy (CBT): Cognitive behavioral therapy (CBT) plays a key part in controlling stress that can drain your mental energy. CBT helps to develop positive cognitive energy by increasing feelings of well-being and clarity. The basis of CBT is learning to be aware of negative thought patterns so you can reorganize those thoughts and behaviors into more affirmative attitudes. A better, more focused mental outlook leads to a sustained increase in mental energy levels.

6. Mindfulness: Mindfulness is an invaluable tool that helps to reduce stress and anxiety through learning to focus on the moment and take in one's feelings and thoughts without any judgment. Mindfulness meditation helps by developing a nonsensitive connection with otherwise strong emotions. This can free up mental energy for use in other success-oriented tasks.

7. Self-Hypnosis for Success: This is a method of entering into a relaxed, aware, and focused state of mind independently, in which you can manage stress, anxiety, and make desirable changes in your life that can also increase your sense of well-being as well as boost mental energy. Through self-hypnosis, you can achieve greater self-confidence in accomplishing goals and achieving personal success.

8. Spirituality: Developing noble traits within your internal self leads to higher self-esteem, happiness, and a greater sense of well-being. A university study found that daily expressions of trust in a power outside one's self increase love for self and charity for others. When we make authentic efforts to improve ourselves, we will develop greater influence with others that can help us achieve our goals.

9. Relationships: Key factors in your relationships that generate increased mental energy are found in feelings of belonging, being accepted, and being liked or loved. You may find individual validation in personal and work associations. You feel trusted and have mutual respect among friends. Deeper relationships are also based upon these and other positive principles. Together, they form a psychological safety net that encourages honesty and taking risks, free from the fear of being judged.

10. **Learning:** Engaging in mentally stimulating activities increases motivation, boosts mental energy, maintains brain health, and enhances cognitive function. For example, hobbies that challenge your mind will improve problem-solving skills, increase brain speed, and improve memory. Apply the Success Matrix when you read, listen to self-help audiobooks and podcasts. You will not only expand your knowledge but you also increase your motivation and boost mental energy.

Decisions About Your Success

Each success-boosting method has been proven effective for its ability to **increase mental energy** and **boost the value of your mental currency!**

My promise to you is this: If you start by writing down a few goals, develop your own time management system, and practice visualizing your success, **you will not fail.** And as you learn and practice each of these success tools, you will grow and succeed far beyond your wildest expectations. **You can create your own "gold standard" of mental currency.**

One final thought

Be aware that life sometimes feels like it's picking on you. But don't worry, it isn't. When you focus on obtaining a serious goal, you begin to see interruptions as challenges. And occasionally, an individual's own *self-defeating behavior* is the culprit.

For this purpose, CBT and mindfulness tools are included in this book for the purpose of helping you stop negative thoughts from undermining your success. So, remember:

"Every challenge you face in life becomes the stepping stone forward in your exciting journey to success!"
Robert D. Hutchings

Chapter Three

GOAL SETTING

How Goal Setting Increases Success

A study conducted by the Harvard Business School demonstrated conclusively that people who set goals experienced ten times more success than non-goal setters (McCormack, 2014). When you set goals, your brain responds in several ways to reward you for taking action. This response triggers increased mental energy, the fuel that drives success!

Here are seven of the cognitive rewards you may experience:

1. **Dopamine response:** The process of setting actionable goals releases dopamine in your brain. It is a "feel-good" neurotransmitter that boosts motivation, pleasure, and that feeling of accomplishment that keeps us coming back for more.

2. **Anxiety reduction response:** The act of setting goals helps to replace negative thinking and anxiety with productive activities. As you

focus on your desired achievements, stress diminishes and you feel in control and mentally energized.

3. **Sense of direction & purpose response:** Goals map out your desired direction to provide direction and purpose in your life. You focus your increased mental energy on achieving your goals rather than wasting life aimlessly looking for purpose.

4. **Improved motivation response:** Your drive to succeed is increased as you make forward progress in setting and achieving your goals, regardless of whether they are huge or small. Success pushes you forward toward more success and fuels your mental energy in the process.

5. **Sense of achievement response:** Accomplishing any goal, whether large or small, increases your sense of achievement, your feeling of self-confidence, and your mental energy. You are more confident and feel more capable of setting and achieving more amazing and challenging goals.

6. **Increased ability to focus response:** As you focus on your desired goal, you push unwanted distractions and needless tasks

aside. Becoming goal-oriented in the process, you maintain higher levels of focused mental energy.

7. **Improved resilience response:** You become more capable of managing problems and challenges in pursuit of your goals. You see obstacles as transitory instead of feeling overwhelmed by them, and you experience increased mental energy to meet the demands of achieving your goals.

Write Down Your Goals

It is critical to get goals out of your head. Write them down on paper or in a digital format. When you write your goals down, they take on lives of their own. They become real, life-altering moments in your life. Perhaps you wonder if this will really happen to you. Yes, it will! Researchers have shown that putting pen to paper activates brain cells, and you literally become different from that point forward.

Putting your goals in black and white is *a requisite first step* **toward success.** Without writing down goals, they are just hoped-for desires. Remember the old Chinese proverb regarding the importance of a first step: "*A journey of a thousand miles begins with a single step,*" attributed to Lao Tzu in *Tao Te Ching*.

The concept is that a successful journey must have a **starting point**, regardless of any daunting challenges that may exist. The proverb illustrates that **big goals are achieved through small steps**. Momentum is built through **consistent and intentional action** that occurs over time. As you **build confidence** through taking this first step and each additional step, your self-confidence, motivation, and mental energy are imbued with **power from within** to achieve every goal and realize long-term success.

Five benefits of writing goals down on paper:

1. **A proven method for success:** *Higher completion rates.* It has been shown that when individuals write down their goals, those individuals are more successful in achieving their goals. *Why write them down?* Because this is one of the most powerful success tools you will ever use.

2. **Increase focus:** *Clarity.* Turns thoughts into well-defined purposes. *Visually* reminds you of the dream you want to achieve.

3. **Enhance accountability & motivation:** *Memory.* Keeps cognitive processes active so goals are processed for long-term memory and recall. As you review your goals daily or weekly, you become accountable for staying motivated

and on task.

4. **Enhance planning:** By writing down goals, you can break them down into chunks, smaller steps, and sub-steps. Using a structured approach such as the 3P *Approach* (Premise, Parts, Procedures), you can *develop detailed plans* to achieve each of your goals.

5. **Accountability's effect:** Individuals who included a friend in their written goal planning as a form of accountability were far more successful in reaching their goals. The creation of a *"goal community"* creates added layers for your personal motivation.

Goal-Setting Theory

In the 1960s, 1990, and 2002, two psychologists, E. A. Locke and G. P. Latham, expanded the elements of goal-setting theory. Today, their work is the foundation of modern goal setting. Their extensive studies and work found that goals that were specific and demanding stirred greater performance than those that were simple, vague, or ambiguous.

Here are key elements of their goal-setting theory:

Specific and difficult: Difficulty is an effective form of motivation. For example, compare these two goals: "*Improve overall productivity 24 percent for the year*" vs. "*We will do our best for the year.*" It's easy to see which goal is both *specific* and *difficult*.

Commitment and ability: An individual's commitment to achieving a goal must also include their ability to realize the goal; the goal must be realistic.

Five values: Goal theory states that these five values must be part of setting a viable goal in order for it to be successfully achieved:

1. **Clarity:** Clear, specific, measurable.

2. **Challenge:** Demanding but not impossible.

3. **Commitment:** Person should accept and approve of the goal.

4. **Feedback:** Necessary to track and adjust.

5. **Complexity:** Break into large, complex, smaller, and sub-goals.

Next, let's evaluate the key elements included in five of the most popular goal-setting methods successful people are using: SMART Goals, Objectives and Key Results (OKRs), WOOP, HARD Goals, and Big Hairy Audacious Goals (BHAGs).

1. SMART Goals. This is a popular goal-setting tool and a widely used framework. SMART stands for *Specific, Measurable, Achievable, Relevant, and Time-bound.*

- **Specific:** Goal must be stated clearly and well-defined. Addresses who, where, when, what, and why.

- **Measurable:** Must be a trackable goal with quantifiable data or metrics in order to know how you are progressing and when you reach your goal.

- **Achievable:** Must be a realistic goal that can be achieved in terms of your available time and resources.

- **Relevant:** Must be a goal that is aligned with your long-term concerns and priorities.

- **Time-bound:** Must have a deadline that creates a feeling of urgency that keeps you on track.

2. **Objectives and Key Results (OKRs).** A goal-setting method popularized by Google that comprises two primary parts.

- **Objectives:** Define the qualities of each goal you desire to achieve in detail. It might look something like this: "*Become the leader among my peers and the global market for the development of creative, cloud-based IT software solutions.*"

- **Key Results (KRs):** Measurable, qualitative

metrics must be used to establish objective measurable results for the established objective. An example could be "*Advance IT software market share from 17 percent to 34 percent within the next 12 months.*"

3. WOOP (Wish, Outcome, Obstacle, Plan). A science-backed method that uses positive mental attitude and honesty regarding reality.

- **Wish:** Recognize an essential, realistic, and doable goal.

- **Outcome:** Visualize your most desired result and how you will feel when you achieve it.

- **Obstacle:** Discern any inner obstacles that may keep you from achieving your goal. These could be feelings, habits, or experiences that may be motivational obstacles.

- **Plan:** (If-Then Plan) Develop a plan to overcome obstacles as they may occur. For example, "*If I catch myself procrastinating when I get home, then I will immediately go to work on my homework.*" Your *If-then* plan should be prepared in advance.

4. BHAGs (Big Hairy Audacious Goals). This is a term created by Jim Collins and Jerry Porras in their book *Built To Last*, which describes visionary, long-term goals that challenge and inspire organizations and individuals.

- **BHAGs:** These are clear, fascinating, and frequently irrational goals when first explained. For example, Elon Musk's goal for humans to land on Mars.

- **Long Term:** Usually, these goals extend over 15-30 years and require the commitment of a unified group of people toward reaching a climactic completion.

5. HARD Goals: These goals are based upon the emotional commitment to accomplish momentous achievements.

- **Heartfelt:** Must be about something you personally care about deeply.

- **Animated:** You must be able to visualize how it will look and how it will feel.

- **Required:** Must have an urgent, immutable feel about completing this goal.

- **Difficult:** Must challenge personal growth and move you outside your comfort zone.

Motivators and Rewards

In order to ascertain your personal **motivation** and **reward** system, you may want to begin thinking about what gets you motivated and how you like to be rewarded for your hard work. Think about internal and external motivation and rewards.

- Example of **internal** motivations & rewards: purpose, self-esteem, passion, personal growth, or experience.

- Example of **external** motivations & rewards: recognition, financial gain, education, or employment.

Additional helpful ways to develop your motivators:

- **Reflect on values:** Write down your core values as a start.

- **Identify passions:** What interests and activities get you energized?

- **Consider strengths:** What strengths can you apply to tasks?

- **Inspiration:** Ask others how they have accomplished similar tasks.

- **Learning & challenges:** Is your motivation taking on new challenges?

Helpful ways to develop *rewards* for reaching each milestone: Reward yourself for the progress you make—perfection not required. However, you should not reward bad behavior such as procrastination.

- Things that appeal to you
- Meaningful rewards
- Try different rewards
- Financial
- Emotional
- Physical
- Recognition

Write down your personal internal and external motivators for setting and achieving challenging goals. Your rewards list is for reaching each new milestone toward your goal. They may be as simple as enjoying your favorite meal, taking a swim, or social time with friends. By breaking goals down into lesser tasks, you may discover improved motivation and commitment.

Conclusion

It's time now to select your method for setting goals, such as SMART goals, and take your next step toward success. Every tool provided in *Your Personal Success Tool Kit* works best when you have at least one solid goal identified, written down, and broken down into smaller chunks or steps toward achievement.

If you have already established solid goals, that's great! However, if not, you should take time now to write down and dissect at least one solid, achievable SMART goal.

Without having written goals, your progress toward success will be hit or miss. Without goals, you may find yourself out of gas, sputtering along with no purpose or direction. Don't procrastinate! It is easier than you think.

The **incredible benefits** that come with having at least one BHAG are the huge boost in **self-confidence** and the **feel-good brain chemicals** that increase *mental energy*. Your motivation will continue to grow and expand with the achievement of each smaller step toward your BHAG.

And as you begin to apply the personal success tools found in this and future chapters, your journey to success will become even more amazing!

Chapter Four

TIME MANAGEMENT METHODS

Misconceptions About Time Management

When you hear the term "Time Management," what comes to mind? Being organized or staying busy? Perhaps you perceive it as becoming perfect in scheduling your productivity, or maybe a system that cuts out breaks? Some might even believe that time management is about being early and staying late every single day. In fact, none of these descriptions is really accurate.

Common misconceptions about time management:

- **Multitasking increases one's productivity**

Many people believe that multitasking is a great way to improve their productivity. However, they would be wrong. Modern studies show that the practice of multitasking is quite the opposite. It actually decreases productivity, increases errors, and decreases mental clarity (Rubinstein et al., 2001).

FACT: Your brain's wiring can only focus on a single task at any one time. Constantly changing attention between several tasks simultaneously will lead to inefficiency, burnout, and decreased mental energy.

- **Being busy equals being productive**

We all know individuals who fill their days with a spectrum of tasks in order to appear busy. However, this does not always mean they are being productive.

FACT: Good time management prioritizes tasks and achievements that are focused on achieving goals. It also includes adequate time to reflect, assess progress, and creatively resolve problems and challenges.

- **Everything is always a "PRIORITY"**

You may have worked for a company where every project and task was stamped as "PRIORITY" and the explanation was that accomplishing the company's mission requires it. When this occurs, there is no true priority because it does not exist. Although the task or project is to be treated as a "PRIORITY," such practices do not always increase productivity.

FACT: Identifying and concentrating on high-impact projects and tasks is the key to effective time management. For example, using the Pareto analysis or 80/20 method, we understand that 80 percent of the best results are generated by just 20 percent of our efforts.

- **Achieving perfection in everything**

Striving for perfection whenever or wherever it is possible is a positive desire with some negative side effects. Striving for perfection in every detail leads to burnout, loss of efficiency, insufficient mental energy, and makes every task or project highly stressful.

FACT: Real time management is focused on creating balance between acceptable timelines and quality. This may mean being more tolerant of human imperfection. Even when using AI or computer-assisted robotic equipment for production, engineers build in tolerances for imperfection.

- **A "one-size-fits-all" attitude**

Many believe that time management comes in a box as a one-size-fits-all solution to managing daily activities. This is not reality. Effective time management methods come in a variety of sizes and shapes to meet the needs of every human personality.

FACT: Methods for successful time management are flexible, easy to personalize, and invaluable tools for success. You can develop a customized time management system focused on your personality, needs, and goals in as little as thirty minutes.

- **I don't want to "punch in and out"**

There is a mentality that perceives time management as a highly controlled system that demands precision time-keeping. This is an old myth held over from England's apprenticeship cast system. Implementing a good method for time management was never meant to be like a shadow looking over your shoulder all day to ensure you are busy every minute of the day.

FACT: Effective time management methods have been proven to *increase* free time. You will not feel as if you are clocking in or out or being controlled by an external force. Rather, a time management method will help you eliminate distractions that otherwise steal your valuable time.

- **Time management means eliminating breaks**

Many seem to think that employing a time management system will cause them to focus only on productive work and eliminate free time. However, when speaking about time management methods, the goal is to increase our time to plan, dream, create, and refresh ourselves during periods of productivity.

FACT: Planning and managing your time resources are important factors in the success of any goal-oriented project. Enjoying needed breaks for some refreshment, lavatory, meals, or simply to stretch your legs is not limited to a good plan. Taking adequate breaks reduces stress, anxiety, and burnout, and increases mental energy.

The truth is that effective time-management techniques are totally noninvasive, goal-friendly, and energy-boosting tools for success.

Time Management for Success

Your success in whatever you do will be positively or negatively impacted, depending on how well you manage your time. Consider these two scenarios:

Positive Impact: When you adopt a good time management technique, you feel a sense of being in control. Research tells us that those feelings of being in control flood the brain with feel-good chemicals that reduce stress, relieve anxiety, and eliminate overwhelm. It causes mental energy to skyrocket to new highs, which directly affects your goal-achievement success.

Negative Impact: Poor time management practices result in feelings of depression from constantly feeling behind in your goal-achievement plan. This brings on stress and anxiety as you ruminate over incomplete, unrealized goals. Ultimately, you find yourself on the verge of burnout, energy drained, enthusiasm stagnating, and mental fog instead of clarity. That's not all. You face sleepless nights, relationship problems, low or no motivation, and drained energy. *You may even think your pilot light has gone out!*

Whether you are an entrepreneur or simply on a journey of self-discovery, here are six energy-increasing reasons for adopting the right time management method:

- **Reduce anxiety and stress**
- **Enhance confidence and productivity**
- **Support healthy habits**
- **Boost self-discipline**
- **Inspire work-life stability**
- **Avoid burnout**

Time Management Methods

Here are nine proven time management methods that may be helpful in creating a plan that works best for your needs. Each method's description includes a suggestion as to the type of individual who may benefit from that particular method. Whether you fit into a suggested personality category or not, it may be worthwhile to learn about each of these nine methods. And who knows, you may develop your own method for managing time after learning what others have done.

1. PARETO ANALYSIS OR 80/20 METHOD

Developed by Italian Vilfredo Pareto, the 80/20 method presents the concept that 80 percent of the outcomes result from 20 percent of the actions. His analysis will assist you in prioritizing those actions most effective for problem-solving. The individuals who may benefit most from the 80/20 method are *analytical thinkers*.

How the Pareto 80/20 method works:

1. **Make a list of challenges you are facing.** An example might be that you are procrastinating with respect to the completion of an important task.

2. **Identify the basic cause of the problem.** Perhaps you are not getting anything completed because you get hyperfocused scrolling through social media or movies.

3. **Add a numerical value to problems.** Give higher numbers to your most important tasks and lower numbers to less important tasks.

4. **Combine problems in groups according to cause.** Group problems together that are caused by hyperfocus, such as scrolling through social media.

5. **Add up the numbers for each group.** That group (issue) with the highest number is the one to work on first.

6. **Get started.** Taking action is often the 20 percent solution.

2. POMODORO METHOD

Created by Francesco Cirillo, this method breaks work down into timed work intervals. The segments are referred to as Pomodoro and are named after Cirillo's tomato-shaped timer. The individuals who may benefit most from the Pomodoro method are *creative thinkers* or *anyone needing to work or study* despite being tired.

How the Pomodoro technique works:

1. Select your task to be completed.

2. Using your timer, select a time length such as twenty-five minutes.

3. Make your focus only on the selected task.

4. When your timer buzzes, stop and keep track of the segment.

5. With the buzzer, it is time to take a five-minute break. Get up, walk around, get a drink—let your brain rest from working on the task.

6. Steps 2–5 should be repeated. After four sessions, start taking longer breaks of twenty-five or thirty minutes.

This method helps you learn a time management skill as well as how to set and achieve goals. It's a great tool for use with a daily or weekly schedule. You'll be able to better stick to your schedules.

3. EISENHOWER MATRIX METHOD

During World War II, Dwight Eisenhower commanded the Allied Forces. In 1953, he became president of the United States of America. Faced with many difficult choices and decisions daily, he developed the Eisenhower Matrix or Urgent vs. Important matrix method of time management. The Eisenhower method is for *critical thinkers* or *people in leadership roles.*

How the Eisenhower method works:

Start by organizing your list of tasks into four different quadrants of a square. The top two boxes of the square are "*Important/Urgent*" (top left box) and "*Important/Nonurgent*" (top right). Tasks assigned to the "Important/Urgent" box are "*Do Right Away*" tasks. Those assigned to "Important/Nonurgent" are "*To Be Decided.*" Urgent tasks are those that need to be completed immediately. Important tasks are those things that add value to your long-term goals, such as making decisions.

Tasks assigned to the lower two boxes of the quadrant are "*Unimportant/Urgent*" (bottom left) and "*Unimportant/Nonurgent*" tasks (bottom right of the quadrant). Note that those tasks assigned to the "Unimportant/Urgent" box are "*To Be Delegated*" while tasks assigned to the "Unimportant/Nonurgent" box are "*To Be Deleted.*"

4. PARKINSON'S LAW METHOD

Cyril Northcote Parkinson, a British historian, spun the phrase "Work expands so as to fill the time available for its completion." His perspective was that the amount of time you plan for yourself to finish a given task is usually the same measure of time it takes for you to finish the task. Individuals who may benefit most from Parkinson's law are *procrastinators* and *people who work well under pressure*.

How Parkinson's law method works:

Although this is not actually a time management method or tool per se, you can put this to work as a time management tool that is very beneficial to your success. By working in short bursts of time, you are efficiently applying this law. This includes helpful tips.

- **Work without your computer charger.** You will be amazed at how quickly you can complete a project before your battery dies.

- **Get things done early.** Rather than waiting until 10 p.m. to complete an assignment, try having it finished by lunchtime.

- **Give yourself a solid deadline.** Allow yourself sufficient time to accomplish a task or project, but cut that time in half.

- **Limit the time to complete certain tasks.** Limit your time for checking and answering texts and emails to just thirty minutes per day.

5. TIME BLOCKING METHOD

Elon Musk is the inventor of this method designed for productivity. Musk's time blocking method helped him work 80 hours per week while having adequate personal time. The time blocking method is best for *working students or parents,* and *analytical thinkers.* Here is his secret.

How the time blocking method works:

Begin by assigning every daily task a time block in which to accomplish that task. For example, eating breakfast, brushing your teeth, or doing your morning workout.

1. **Create two columns on a piece of paper.** In the first column, you will write each hour of your

day in half-hour chunks, adding specific time blocks you have created for yourself.

2. **Decide the amount of time a task will take.** Write that task in the opposite column across from the time chunks and fit them into your schedule.

3. **Allow some buffer time between blocks.** Allow yourself to adjust your time blocks to best meet your time.

6. GETTING THINGS DONE METHOD (GTD)

David Allen is the author of this time management technique. You write down those things you wish to accomplish on a piece of paper, then reduce each item to an actionable task. The GTD method is best for *those who have difficulty focusing on only one task at a time* and *those who are overwhelmed in daily life.*

How the GTD method works:

1. **Record the thoughts and actions receiving your attention:** These are your work, school, or personal tasks that have your attention.

2. Clarify their meaning: Are these actionable tasks? If not, ignore the item at present. If actionable, get it done, hand it off to someone else to complete, or set it aside for another day.

3. **Arrange your actions:** According to your needs, prioritize the list of items you need to accomplish.

4. **Reflection:** Cross tasks off the list as they are completed, and review the list often to determine the next task or project with priority.

5. **Begin:** Engage in action to complete lesser tasks that can be completed now.

7. RAPID PLANNING METHOD (RPM)

This method was developed by Tony Robbins. It is a method for training the brain to envision the things you want to accomplish. In theory, RPM stands for "result, purpose, and massive action." Those who will benefit most from RPM are *working students or parents*, and *those with long-term goals*.

How the RPM works:

1. **Capturing:** Make a written list of all tasks to complete during the week.

2. **Chunking:** "Chunk" tasks together by their common associations, such as work, school, personal life, or special projects.

3. **Create personal RPM blocks:** On a sheet of paper, create three columns: The task

to complete, the result you want, plus the purpose and the action you will take to accomplish it.

4. **Create your empowering role:** An example of this might be to call yourself "the boss" if you own the company. The role is to help you get energized to help you focus on completing the task.

8. PICKLE JAR THEORY METHOD

The pickle jar theory will help you discern the useful from the unuseful things in your life. You will be able to plan tasks, enjoy your spare time, and set daily priorities more easily. The two types of individuals who will find this method valuable are *visual people* and *creative thinkers*.

How the Pickle Jar Theory works:

Imagine or visualize a glass pickle jar filled to the top with rocks, pebbles, and sand. The bigger rocks are on the bottom, the smaller pebbles are on top of the rocks, and sand fills in around the rocks from bottom to top.

1. **The Rocks:** Your most important tasks of the day to get done.

2. **The Pebbles:** Tasks to be done that can be finished another day.

3. **The Sand:** The disruptions, such as text messages, phone calls, and email.

As you begin to plan your day, consider your tasks and categorize each one according to the descriptions above. Create a list that starts with rocks, then add the pebbles, and finally pour in the sand. Plan adequate time for each item on your list. It is suggested that you not plan more than six hours of projects during an eight-hour day to leave a buffer for the pebbles and sand.

9. EAT THAT FROG METHOD

Named after a Mark Twain quote: **"Eat a live frog first thing in the morning and nothing worse will happen to you the rest of the day."** Your day begins by first doing the most difficult tasks. This allows you to move on to your less energy-consuming tasks of the day and so on. The best frog eater types are *abstract thinkers* and *those with long-term goals.*

How the Eat That Frog method works:

Write down your goals:

1. **Clarify your goals:** What are the most onerous tasks to get out of the way?

2. **Write down your goals:** Add details to describe what your goal looks like.

3. **Set realistic deadlines:** Build in extra time to account for unforeseen problems.

4. **Complete a list:** Make a list of things you must do to reach your goals.

5. **Prioritize your list:** The most important goal-oriented tasks are the "frogs."

6. **Start with action:** More than one frog on the list? Eat your nastiest frog first.

7. **Review and repeat daily:** Consistently move forward toward your goals.

Conclusion

It doesn't matter if you are a student, an entrepreneur gaining new skills, a manager developing improved skills, or a working parent going back to school, developing good time management skills is vital to your success. Here are some suggestions to help you get started.

If your habit is to put things off and wait until time is short to get things done, you may benefit from trying *eat that frog* or *Parkinson's law* time management methods. Those who have difficulty staying focused or working for long periods of time on a task will find the *Pomodoro technique* extremely helpful because it allows you to focus or work intensely for short intervals of time, then take a break.

Regardless of which time management method you find most helpful, you will benefit from a boost in self-esteem and self-confidence, increased motivation, and the determination to achieve long-term success. Developing time management skills will truly multiply your personal success and prosperity throughout your life.

Tip: Consider writing a positive affirmation statement (see Chapter 6) focused on the positive application of a good time management method.

Chapter Five

VISUALIZATION

What Visualization Is and How It Works

Visualization is the act of creating mental images within your imagination in order to simulate scenarios, experiences, and events. **Visualization is a cognitive dry run** during which emotions, thoughts, and behaviors are rehearsed, and real-life neural pathways are activated. Visualization is linked to increased mental energy.

Repetition is the key to successfully employing visualization to achieve success. As you develop and improve your skill in visualizing achieving goals and success, you will also increase your self-confidence, motivation, and self-esteem. And you will gain tremendous personal power. You will be able to **precondition your mind and body** to perform and achieve at extraordinary levels of success.

Visualization as a strategy for increasing your mental energy may become one of your favorite strategies due to its far-reaching benefits. Every time you create mental images of the success you are seeking, skills you are trying to develop, or dreams you wish to bring to life, you are creating real memories. Let me repeat that: **You are creating real memories** as if you have already accomplished those images.

Here is an overview of the features of visualization:

1. Mental Rehearsal Expands Neural Pathways

As you intensely visualize an action, neural pathways associated with that action are created and strengthened in your brain. This is called *mental rehearsal*. You can apply mental rehearsal to enhance and expand task performance as well as create improved mental scripts. This technique is used extensively in pro sports, theatre, and even by motivational speakers.

The process is simple. You **train your brain to heighten your thoughts, movements, and actions** involved in a desired task or behavior through repetitively visualizing your entire performance. This is the technique used by athletes to prepare for competition and musicians use to mentally practice prior to concerts.

2. Your Mind-Body Connection

Visualization triggers neural pathways that cause a physical response in your body that is comparable to a real-life experience. An example of this might be visualizing that you are in a peaceful, calm setting. As you persist in visualizing your peaceful environment, you begin to feel relaxed, less stressed, and breathe more slowly.

In comparison, if you visualize being in a high-stress environment, you might notice that your body reacts with increased muscle tension and a rising heart rate. The point is that **there is a definite mind-body connection** that underscores visualizations' influence on your emotional and physical condition.

3. The Emotional Influence of Mental Images

It's interesting to note that your mental images during visualization exercises can often deeply affect your emotions. When you experience positive imagery, feelings of confidence, happiness or motivation may accompany it. Conversely, negative images may evoke stress, anxiety, or anger. Thus, when you choose mental images that are empowering and positive, you will **create an affirmative state that increases feelings of well-being**, which increases your mental energy.

4. Programming Your Subconscious Mind

Your subconscious mind does not know the difference between things that are real and things that are not real, or your purposefully created mental images. The exciting part of the subconscious mind is that it will believe whatever you tell it.

As desired outcomes are visualized, your subconscious mind believes they're presently happening. This motivates you to achieve your goals and turn your mental images into reality. This also programs your subconscious to do what is needed in order to attract success.

5. Practical Applications

Visualization is a versatile technique that can be applied to various areas of life, including sports, business, personal development, and overcoming challenges. As you incorporate repetitive visualization into your self-help routine, you will harness a powerful tool to help you achieve greater goals and live an abundant life.

Benefits of Visualization

The skill of visualization or mental imagery is developed as you repeatedly tap into your physiological and psychological neuropathways. This is **a powerful self-help tool** that requires high levels of mental energy to function, and that also replenishes your mental energy levels.

Visualization is a strategy that works well in conjunction with every strategy that boosts cognitive energy and is an indispensable tool for personal success!

Five benefits of visualization:

1. Neuroplasticity and neural pathway activation.

The process of visualizing a particular activity, process, or goal will train your brain how to perform the desired activities. Similar levels of neurotransmitters are called up for the learning process. The best part is that as you practice visualization, the brain develops more efficiency in processing data and reacting to future situations that are similar. Because of this, your brain increases your mental energy from not working with unfamiliar scenarios.

2. Reduced stress and anxiety.

Visualization exercises involving positive or peaceful environments activate the body's parasympathetic nervous system, which can result in a relaxation response. This state reduces cortisol and delivers a sense of well-being from the lack of stress or anxiety. This increases your mental energy level, which in turn enables greater creativity, focus, and cognitive tasks.

3. Increased motivation and focus.

Visualizing goal achievement and overcoming challenges is a powerful personal motivator. Positive visualization sessions on a regular basis reinforce your growing capacity to focus and attain goals. It also boosts faith in your personal power to achieve success. Increased motivation coupled with better focus translates to increased mental energy and determination to achieve your dreams.

4. Boosted self-confidence.

Self-confidence and self-belief are positively impacted by regular practice of visualization. As you mentally rehearse positive outcomes, you can also program to improve self-confidence and self-belief with a positive can-do attitude. As you discover your new self-assurance and confidence, you will also gain greater goal-focused energy that will be unstoppable.

5. Enhanced emotional regulation.

Visualization will help you gain a much better emotional compass while engaging a nonreactive attitude regarding emotion. This approach engages mindfulness within your visualization to prevent you from being carried away into emotional battles caused by challenges. Use your visualization skills to improve your goal achievement, as well as a self-help tool to become a better version of yourself.

Visualization to Combat Mental Fatigue

Mental fatigue is a fact of life. Effective visualization skills can be awesome tools with which to combat fatigue. It shifts your mental frame of mind, decreases stress and accompanying anxiety, and refreshes your clarity of mind.

Outlined here are five visualization strategies plus three tips specially created to revitalize mental fatigue and boost your mental energy. These exercises are also very useful when practicing meditation or self-hypnosis.

1. Guided Imagery: Natural Serene Settings

Technique: Can you imagine yourself being in one of nature's most peaceful and relaxing environments where you can engage each of your senses? Perhaps you create the imagery of being on a tranquil, white, sandy beach with the sound of waves, or in a lush, green forest listening to the small animals and birds, or perhaps next to a high mountain lake with crystal blue water.

How it helps: Transporting yourself to a peaceful location during visualization can help reduce stress, anxiety, and hormones like cortisol. The point is that those emotions and hormones cause mental fatigue and rob your mental energy. Take a restorative break to recharge your energy and rest your mind.

2. The Pathway to Clarity

Technique: Imagine walking along a beautiful pathway covered with fog, and with every step, you feel your mental fog and your worries clear away, and the path becomes clear and easy to see. At the end of the path, you come to an open area and can see clearly for miles around, and begin to feel an understanding of your clarity of mind.

How it helps: This method is meant to help you clear away mental clutter and refresh your focus using visualization. As you move forward through the fog into clarity, you let go of those things that are causing the fog. It helps to create mental freedom and renew your clarity and purpose.

3. Clearing the Fog with Breathing

Technique: Locate a quiet place to breathe. As you breathe in several deep breaths and blow the air out slowly, pay attention to the sensation of breathing. Similar to clarity, visualize the ground covered in a light fog, which represents mental fatigue, distractions, and stress. As you walk through the fog, breathe in, and as you breathe out, imagine the fog beginning to go away and leaving a clear area where you are standing. Breathe in comfortably and enjoy your clarity as the fog dissipates.

How it helps: This method uses deep breathing and visualization to help you clear away mental fatigue and clutter. As you move forward through the fog into clarity, you let go of those things that are causing the fog. It helps to refresh mental energy and renew your clarity and purpose.

4. Problem-Solving with Clarity

Technique: When you are struggling with a particular problem that is causing mental fatigue, try visualizing that problem being placed in a cardboard box, placing the lid on the box, then setting the box aside. Step away from the box and view the box containing that problem.

In your mind's eye, visualize a wise old mentor coming to your side and starting a mental dialogue with them about potential solutions. Visualize positive outcomes and change negative thoughts or feelings to positive emotions as you resolve mental fatigue and feel your mental energy returning.

How it helps: The box technique helps to separate your emotion from the problem as you search for creative solutions. Stepping away from the box allows you to let go of feeling bogged down while helping to boost mental energy levels.

5. Your Future Self

Technique: Visualize yourself living an exceptional life in the future. You are living a life of abundant happiness, health, and success. Be sure to include your environment, relationships, and accomplishments. As you engage your future self, ask questions and get advice about how you might accomplish your goals and stay on your path to success.

How it helps: Using this technique will boost your self-confidence and self-esteem. It can produce a clearer view of your direction and eliminate feelings of fatigue or aimlessness in your life. As you create a positive image of your desired future, you create the visual roadmap to guide you from where you are now to your success-filled future. It will create a strong sense of purpose within your brain to increase your mental energy.

6. Tips for Effective Visualization

Engage all your senses: Do not limit your visualized imagery to a silent movie. Include all five senses to create your mental movie. Immerse yourself in a vivid experience.

Regular practice is key: Consistently practice to improve your skills. You should dedicate time each day to exercise your visualization techniques.

Be patient: It takes time to develop visualization skills, so be patient with yourself and don't get discouraged if you feel challenged. As you practice, your ability to experience vivid mental visualization will improve, and you will enjoy the greater benefits promised.

Developing Visualization Skills

Visualize your desired outcome as if it is already occurring, including your emotions and sensations associated with it.

Recap: How to develop visualization skills:

1. Find a quiet space where you can relax without distractions. 2. Plan a goal for visualization. Be clear about what you want to achieve. 3. Engage all your senses; don't just imagine the visual aspect. 4. Practicing regularly is the key to improving your skills. 5. Begin with deep-breathing relaxation exercises as you learn to focus. 6. Make practice a habit, a part of your daily routine. 7. Be patient with yourself because learning to visualize takes time.

Visualization is an unmatched success tool that magnifies your mental energy, motivation, commitment, and self-confidence beyond any benchmark along the pathway to success. I recommend you embrace visualization as your "go-to" success tool and couple it with other tools for an even greater impact.

Chapter Six

POSITIVE AFFIRMATIONS

Introduction to Positive Affirmations

The two most frequently asked questions about positive affirmations are: "**What are positive affirmations?**" and "**How can they help me?**" Very simply put, a positive affirmation consists of **an affirming statement** focused on bringing about positive change(s) in your life. **Affirmations** describe the action you are performing presently in order to create positive new behavior or to replace unwanted negative behavior.

Traditional positive affirmations are written statements in which you describe the thing you are seeking for self-improvement: i.e., behaviors, goals, health, finances, or accomplishments. Using positive affirmations engages the universe and your subconscious mind, both helping you obtain those things you tell it you want.

It is important that your positive affirmation statements are written using only positive language.

You should **never include negative words** (such as "no", "not", "none", "nothing", "never"), words with negative meanings, connotations, or tones in any affirmation. We will go into more detail about writing affirmations later in the chapter.

Positive affirmations are powerful tools that take advantage of **neuroplasticity to rewire the mind into a positive state.** They work deep down in your subconscious mind, where they eventually become automatic behavior and help align your values and goals.

Through **regular and consistent out loud repetition**, such as each morning or at bedtime, you will feel your desired results becoming a reality in your life. The simple fact many do not understand is that affirmations work silently and powerfully.

The Secret Key to Powerful Affirmations

The Shocking Reality: The world teaches people how to write standard positive affirmations that do absolutely nothing. Traditional versions of positive affirmations do not work because they lack the power to change anything.

Why traditional affirmations don't work: They do not work because all traditional or "worldly" methods of writing positive affirmations lack the secret sauce. YOU are about to be given one of the most valuable self-help secrets you will ever receive! It is the key that will unlock your positive affirmations—turning them into one of the most powerful, success-boosting, personal development tools you will ever own.

The secret key to writing successful affirmations

When writing positive affirmations, you must write them using **present-tense-active language**. I promise that, even if this is the only success-boosting tool you take away from this book, this is worth hundreds of times more than the price of this book!

Why use present-tense-active language

Science has proven that present-tense-active is the *language of the subconscious mind* and the only language that your subconscious mind hears—the only language to which it responds. In order for your affirmations to be effective, they must be heard and absorbed by your subconscious mind.

Thus, the secret key to unlock your success in writing positive affirmations is writing in the language of the subconscious mind or LSM. Research tells us that our subconscious mind will bring us everything we ask for if we ask for it correctly.

The conscious mind

The conscious mind has judgment. Its job is to make decisions and choices. The conscious mind may hear your affirmations, but will not take action because it's already busy doing what it does—thinking about resolving challenges, ruminating about relationships, or making plans for dinner with friends.

The subconscious mind

On the other hand, the subconscious mind has no judgment and accepts everything you tell it as the truth. An interesting research study from the 1920s concluded that the subconscious mind also has access to outside information about which we are unaware.

Many studies since that time have come to similar conclusions. They have concluded that the subconscious mind works quietly in the deep regions of the brain to autonomically control our lives and that it also works to bring us whatever we tell it we need or want in life.

The caveat

Your positive affirmations must be written using LSM, or they will just be an exercise in futility. Read your affirmations out loud frequently and consistently so your subconscious hears them. And remember, you can have whatever you desire in life because your subconscious mind's job is to bring you whatever you tell it you want.

Writing Positive Affirmations

1. When writing affirmations include words that **describe your five senses** (touch, sound, sight, smell, and taste) along with vivid and descriptive images. Use descriptive language to evoke positive feelings, thoughts, and engage your mind and body in realistic sensations. Word images will go right down into your subconscious mind.

2. Select and use powerful descriptive words in your affirmations. Include inner core values, personal strengths, and desired qualities or positive outcomes. Add positive alternatives to replace negative phrasing in affirmations. For example, rather than writing "**I am not gaining weight**," you might write, "**I am becoming more fit and slimmer each day.**"

3. Write specific and personal affirmations rather than generic statements. Adapt affirmation statements to your individual desires, goals, and unique challenges. Write affirmations to **include definite outcomes or actions** and never use vague descriptions.

For example, rather than "**I am working hard each day**," you might write, "**Each and every day, I am completing every assigned and self-assigned task to the best of my ability.**"

4. Include emotion-evoking words and thoughts that link every positive emotion you desire to experience, i.e., happiness, peace, strength, gratitude, or love. An example might be "**I am feeling greater gratitude for my growing success**," or "As I am exercising each and every day, my physical strength is increasing and I am feeling more confident, calm, and energized."

5. **Use action or active words in your affirmations,** such as "**I am feeling**," "**I am becoming**," "**I am achieving**," "**I am doing**," or "**I am choosing**." You are writing active affirmations as though they are occurring each and every time you say them out loud.

Your desired outcome must be paired with action because action reinforces subconscious acceptance of the reality of your affirmations. **Write and think in present-tense-Action.**

6. **Focus on writing** concise and impactful affirmations that are easy to remember and recite. Statements that are easily repeated are better assimilated by your subconscious mind, simpler to memorize, and flow unobstructed into daily planning, activities, and creative thinking. Research tells us that affirmations of five to twelve words are the ideal length.

7. **Consistently repeat affirmations out loud** once, twice, or more times every day. Plan ample time in a comfortable, private space to repeat your affirmations out loud—uninterrupted. Begin the process of reading out loud as soon as you have your first affirmation. You don't need to write every affirmation in order to get

started. Include additional affirmations in your daily routine as you write them.

As you begin using affirmations, know that every affirmation you write will not be perfect at first. **It's a process to fine-tune your affirmations**, so you may find yourself rethinking and rewriting your positive affirmations as you move forward. Make them meaningful, align them with your personal values, and focus on realizing goals.

While **your subconscious mind accepts everything as truth**, you should still keep your affirmations believable. Make positive affirmations part of your daily success routine. Repetition is the key to your success. Reading affirmations out loud reinforces positive neural pathways every time you repeat an affirmation and links your affirmations to real, tangible actions.

Positive Affirmations & Neuroplasticity

Affirmations increase your mental energy levels by tapping into the power of Neuroplasticity within your brain in the following ways:

1. Developing additional neural corridors

Affirmations leverage your brain's power to restructure itself. This is referred to as "neuroplasticity". As you consistently focus on your positive needs and wants through affirmations, your neural corridors or pathways are strengthened. This improves your ability to engage in positive thinking, energy-boosting self-talk, and action-based productivity.

2. Reducing negative neural corridors

As your positive neural corridors become stronger, those corridors or pathways connecting negative thoughts, poor self-confidence, and lack of motivation become weaker. Mental energy levels previously drained by negative thoughts and rumination begin to recover. You will experience increasing mental energy to help achieve positive objectives.

3. Boost in serotonin and dopamine levels

Positive affirmations boost levels of neurotransmitters such as serotonin and dopamine. An increase in "feel-good" chemicals will improve motivation, mood, and feelings of well-being. This correlates with an increase in mental energy levels.

4. Reduction in cortisol levels

Positive affirmations can help reduce the effects of cortisol, the body's stress hormone. Cortisol drains mental energy as it manifests its presence through poor concentration and fatigue. The relaxing effects of positive affirmations lower cortisol levels, improve focus, and increase mental energy levels.

5. Challenging negative thinking

Negative thinking and self-limiting beliefs are cognitively draining. Positive affirmations neutralize and replace negative thoughts and rumination by focusing on those positive actions and behaviors that bring about positive outcomes. Removing unwanted negative thoughts, self-doubt, lack of motivation, and their associated harmful behaviors definitely increases mental energy levels.

6. Expanding growth and learning

Positive affirmations are especially proficient at enhancing and expanding cognitive growth, focus, and learning. Affirmations nurture your ability to creatively solve problems, learn new skills, and expand personal growth. Positive growth inertia expands success while renewing and increasing your mental energy.

7. Developing faith in self

Affirmations continually strengthen faith in your ability to succeed and boost self-efficacy. Faith in yourself strengthens self-confidence, motivation, problem-solving, and boosts mental energy.

8. Empower goal-focused behavior.

Positive affirmations provide a clear-cut conduit focused on achieving your specific goals and behaviors. It's only when you repeatedly and consistently read them out loud that your inner motivation, commitment, and willingness to act take over at the subconscious level to automatically empower your desired new behavior. As you do so, your mental energy will soar even higher.

Perhaps you can see how positive affirmations mold your neuroplastic brain to create cognitive change. Neuroplasticity occurs as our brain creates new neural pathways and diminishes old, unwanted negative neural pathways.

Neuroplasticity is engaged when we boost feel-good chemicals to reduce cortisol, when negative thinking is challenged in order to foster learning and growth, and when we *exercise faith in ourselves* to accomplish BHAG achievements.

Using Positive Affirmations with Visualization

Can you imagine combining positive affirmations with visualization in order to engage all your senses to enjoy a total experience in positive neuroplasticity? Here are four basic strategies for combining positive affirmations with visualization:

1. Guided Imagery and affirmations

Technique: Combine affirmations with guided imagery exercises. For example, while you are visualizing a serene and peaceful garden, you repeat out loud, "*I am feeling peaceful and calm here in my garden.*"**Benefits:** You will strengthen your experience and belief.

2. Vision Boards with affirmations

Technique: Develop your vision board using pictures that represent your goals and the matching affirmations. Be sure to review your board each day and to repeat your affirmations daily. You may also want to pair an image with your affirmation. **Benefits:** This method helps you keep your goals visible while strengthening your commitment via the verbal and visual cues.

3. Journaling visualized affirmations

Technique: Write your positive affirmations, then write a detailed description of what the achievement of each one feels like and looks like, along with your sensory feelings about each affirmation.**Benefits:** Your affirmations and visualizations become linked, which increases your feelings of goal attainability.

4. Mindful deep breathing and affirmations

Technique: Deep breathing, a visualization and mindfulness relaxation technique, combined with positive affirmations. Begin by visualizing the process and performing the process of breathing in positive energy and breathing out doubts and fears. Pair this exercise with an affirmation such as "*More and*

more self-confidence is flowing within me, and doubt and fear are flowing away and disappearing forever."
Benefits: Promotes self-relaxation, strengthens self-confidence, and increases your ability to focus.

Some final thoughts to consider as you begin practicing visualization:

- Ensure that your goals are realistic and specific. Be certain that your affirmations and visualizations are aligned with your personal values.

- You must engage your emotions to tap into your feelings of achieving goals and outcomes.

- Consistency will reprogram your subconscious mind. Make repetition a daily habit because consistency is key to your success.

- Believe that the process works. Trust that you have what it takes to achieve your desires and successes.

- Take action. In the real world, you must actively employ these techniques mentally and physically in order to move toward success, reaching your full potential.

Start now to integrate these proven techniques into your life.

Remember this:

Your life will never be the same again, because you have increased your mental energy. Keep going! Keep working. Keep trying! By stepping forward and working to develop your success skills, you are miles ahead of those who complain about the unfairness of life but do nothing to improve their lot.

Regardless of the pace, stay consistent and focused on achieving your goals and dreams. Have faith in your ability to accomplish every goal you set, because nothing is impossible for you to achieve!

In the next chapter, you will learn about CBT and Mindfulness, two extraordinary personal success tools for turning negative thoughts and feelings into positive thoughts and feelings—**Powerful tools for managing life's challenges.**

Chapter Seven

CBT & MINDFULNESS MEDITATION

How to Use CBT for Personal Success

This book is not meant to be a psychology textbook. However, I have included CBT and mindfulness because they are very effective self-help tools.

This chapter is not meant as an alternative to professional mental health assistance. Rather, understanding CBT and mindfulness will help you analyze negative thoughts (without attachment) and replace those thoughts with positive, productive thoughts that will help you achieve your long-term goals.

Cognitive behavioral therapy (CBT) provides an organized means to recognize and alter thoughts or behaviors that reduce mental energy levels. CBT is grounded in the concept that feelings, thoughts, and actions are interrelated. Let's take a look at six crucial CBT approaches that can help you increase mental energy.

1. Detect and challenge negative patterns of thought

Identify **ANTs (automatic negative thoughts)**. ANTs are the hasty, frequently unhelpful thoughts that dart into your mind. CBT helps you recognize thought patterns such as catastrophizing, self-doubt, or all-or-nothing.

Once patterns are recognized, a process of *cognitive restructuring* is engaged. In this process, you test the accuracy of those thoughts and reframe each one into a more sensible and accurate perspective.

You might also use **a journal to create a "thought record"** to trace your thoughts, feelings, and triggers, and observe progress in replacing ANTs with positive, desirable thoughts. Progress boosts mental energy.

2. Behavioral activation

Schedule and participate in activities that bring you happiness and joy, a sense of accomplishment, and/or pleasure. This behavior will stimulate a positive mood and boost overall motivation, which increases mental energy levels.

We all need recreation in order to release our positive neurotransmitters. Overwhelming tasks should be broken down into smaller, easily managed steps so they become less formidable and improve our probability of success.

Finally, schedule fewer activities at the start of a project. You will gain greater confidence as new activities are added. And as you progressively increase the number and variety of activities in each new project, you will enjoy feelings of success without nagging feelings of overwhelm.

3. Stress management and relaxation exercises

In order to better manage stress, we must first identify what triggers our stress. We need to develop an awareness for situations, activities, or thoughts that cause our stress and mental fatigue.

We do this by mindfully focusing on the present moment when we first experienced stress. Without judgment of our feelings or thoughts, we disengage from the automatic negative thoughts (ANTs). Mindfulness also lessens rumination while also enhancing emotional regulation.

Relaxation exercises for stress reduction include techniques such as progressive muscle relaxation, deep breathing, and visualization. Each of these will help calm your body and mind while reducing stress levels. These relaxation techniques also increase mental energy levels.

4. Improve sleep hygiene

Quality sleep is extremely important to overall physical and cognitive health. Establishing a consistent sleep schedule with regular wake and sleep times, including weekends, helps synchronize your body's clock. Sleep is so important that the U.S. military studied how to help its personnel improve their sleep.

CBT for insomnia particularly targets negative beliefs regarding sleep that interfere with good sleep. One of the first steps for obtaining quality sleep is reviewing your sleep environment. Your bedroom should be dark, cool, and quiet.

Your bedtime routine should include calming activities such as a warm bath, reading, or music to assist your mental preparation for sleep. Turn off all electronic devices thirty to forty-five minutes before sleeping. Poor sleep habits drain mental energy. Sleep is critical to increasing mental energy.

5. Develop successful coping skills

Good coping skills allow you to manage all of your daily activities and stressors successfully without draining mental energy. Some of the skills include **activity pacing**, where you break activities into chunks to prevent overexertion while conserving energy. Activities prioritized according to energy levels also sidestep the "boom or bust" approach that can result in mental energy crashes.

Another tool for coping with mental energy demands is setting boundaries to protect your time and energy. It requires assertiveness and clearly communicating your boundaries. When setting boundaries, be prepared to say "No" in order to protect your availability of positive mental energy.

6. Seek professional help

Practicing CBT for self-help can be most valuable. However, working with a professional counselor or therapist may improve the success of treatment when severe issues persist.

Through the practice of CBT techniques, it's possible to gain control of emotions, thoughts, or even behaviors. This emotional control method leads to reduced mental fatigue and a sense of well-being during challenging times or events in your long-term pursuit of success.

There are numerous self-help resources to assist in learning more about CBT techniques, such as books, apps, websites, and online CBT programs. For now, let's move on to **comparing CBT with Mindfulness**. Both are effective tools for improving mood, motivation, well-being, and increasing mental energy. Yet they differ in their methodology and focus.

How to Use Mindfulness to Increase Motivation

Mindfulness is an invaluable tool to enhance thoughts, emotions, and motivation. It results in feeling less stress, improved focus, and better-regulated emotions. In short, these combined factors boost mental resilience and increase mental energy. Below are six mindfulness approaches that can help increase your mental energy and personal motivation.

1. Stress reduction

When you focus on the current moment and accept thoughts or feelings without judgment, mindfulness assists you in decreasing stress levels. Chronic stress drains mental energy and can bring on doubt about achieving your goals. Alleviating stress frees up mental resources.

This happens as the practice of mindfulness steers us toward reduced activity in our amygdala (the brain's center of fear) and amplified activity in our prefrontal cortex, which is our center for thought responses.

2. Improved focus and attention

Mindfulness techniques, such as mindful meditation, train your brain to pay attention while diminishing distractions. The result is your improved ability to concentrate on regularly performed tasks. This strategy also enables you to achieve increased productivity with greater efficiency while preserving mental energy.

3. Enhance emotional regulation

Mindfulness can help you become aware of your emotions and develop a nonreactive attitude toward them. Rather than being moved by heavy emotions, you observe them and let them pass by naturally. This method of regulating emotion reduces the amount of cognitive energy focused on unwanted emotional battles and frees up mental energy for use on more important, success-oriented tasks.

4. Better sleep quality

If you are among those who experience difficulty sleeping because of rampant thoughts or feelings of anxiety, mindfulness offers you a solution for a better night's sleep. It can calm your mind as you prepare for bed to support a more restful night. A better quality of sleep will increase your mental energy and productivity throughout the day.

5. Reduced rumination

Rumination is your brain's tendency to repeat negative thoughts, feelings, and experiences over and over again. Mindfulness has been shown to be effective in reducing rumination. It does so by promoting an **"in-the-moment consciousness"** that helps you let go of unwanted energy-draining behavior.

6. Increased cognition function

According to modern research, mindfulness practices will enrich your cognitive capabilities. Mindfulness techniques have been shown to improve attention, memory, and cognitive elasticity. This means you will enjoy sharper mental clarity, more resilient recall, and a boost of mental energy.

Compare CBT & Mindfulness

Both CBT and *mindfulness* are very effective and powerful methods for improving mental energy, mood, well-being, and personal motivation. But they are substantially different in methods and primary focus. Let's compare the two techniques for increasing mood, well-being, and cognitive energy.

1. The primary focus of each method

CBT: Focuses on recognizing and changing negative thought patterns and conduct that increase emotional distress with the goal of exchanging those patterns and behaviors in order to improve emotional health, well-being, and overall physical and cognitive energy.

Mindfulness: Works to focus on the current moment and accept thoughts or feelings without judgment to assist you in decreasing stress levels. The goal of mindfulness is to change your relationship with thoughts, versus changing the thought. Mindfulness relieves stress and frees up mental resources to boost mental energy.

2. Examples of how each method approaches thought

CBT: If an individual experiences a challenge and thinks, *I am a failure*, CBT helps them query the thought and select a more positive perspective—reframing thoughts or feelings.

Mindfulness: A practice of fostering one's sense of impartiality from thoughts so they are not judged by their content. Rather than thinking, *I am mad*, the individual might observe, *I have the thought that I'm mad*. Mindfulness allows us to detach our emotional self from challenges. This encourages a sense of well-being, positive mood, and increased energy.

3. Techniques used by CBT and Mindfulness

CBT: Uses the techniques of *behavioral activation, cognition restructuring, relaxation exercises, exposure therapy,* or *thought records*. Relaxation techniques include progressive muscle relaxation and deep breathing.

Mindfulness: Uses *mindful meditation* techniques such as *open monitoring, focused attention, mindful breathing, body scans,* and *mindful movement* (similar to yoga or tai chi). Meditation is an excellent tool for boosting our sense of well-being and cognitive energy levels.

4. Goals and outcomes of each modality

CBT: Provides useful skills and approaches for managing stress, emotions, and resolving daily-life problems.

Mindfulness: Fosters in-the-moment awareness, nurturing self-compassion, promoting inner peace and self-acceptance, and decreasing reactivity.

In conclusion, **CBT and mindfulness both offer you invaluable strategies** to advance your feelings of well-being, improve mood, increase motivation, and stay focused on long-term success.

Mindfulness Meditation Techniques

An obscure concept founded by Buddhist monks some 500 years before Christ was born, mindful meditation has been adopted into today's personal development domain.

Mindfulness meditation has been shown to substantially increase mental energy levels while providing other healthful benefits to those who practice meditation. According to several studies, participants reported less fatigue, reduced anger, lowered anxiety, fewer depressive symptoms, stress relief, and decreased stress-related cortisol.

To help you get started, here are five mindfulness meditation techniques to try out:

1. Focused breathing (mindful breathing) is a keystone of meditation techniques.

Technique: Sit comfortably with eyes closed. Breathe normally and become aware of the sensations of breathing as you breathe in and out. Focus on the feeling of air moving in and out of your lungs and the movement of your chest with each breath in and out. In the beginning, as your mind may wander (and it naturally will). Gently guide your mind back to focusing on breathing.

If you have never meditated before, you may want to begin with shorter 10-minute sessions and work up to longer sessions as you feel more confident. As you use the focused breathing method to meditate for longer periods of time, begin to notice how you feel during and after your meditation session.

Benefits: There is no judgment as you practice this technique. Your repetition in focusing and redirecting your mind back to your breathing strengthens your ability to keep your focus on a task or object. Much like training a muscle, as you exercise your attention, it becomes stronger.

You will soon tune out external sounds, your body will feel refreshed, your mind will become energized, and you will enjoy greater clarity.

2. Body scan meditation is a versatile technique that is also useful in self-hypnosis.

Technique: Lie comfortably on your back on the floor, bed, or couch. Or, if more comfortable, you could sit in a chair with your back straight. Begin by closing your eyes and becoming aware of your feet and toes. The technique is to move your attention from one body part to the next as you move from toes to the top of your head (or from head to toes).

For example, starting at your toes, scan your feet, then your ankles, shins, calves, knees, and so forth (scan both legs together rather than individually).

As you scan each body part, become aware of how it feels. Then tell that body part to relax and scan the next body part. Upon arriving at the top of your head, all of your body should be very relaxed.

In the beginning, your mind may wander (and it naturally will). Gently guide your focus back to the body part being scanned, and move forward until your body scan is complete. As you practice body scan meditation, you will become proficient at achieving total relaxation.

Benefits: Through body scan meditation, you give each body part the command to **"Let go and relax"** as you focus upon it. This technique helps you develop the mental ability to control the body.

In addition, you can identify tension within your body, learn to let go of it, and replace it with relaxation. As you shift your focus systematically, you strengthen concentration and your ability to focus without being interrupted by needless thoughts or rumination.

After practicing body-scan meditation, you will come to feel as physically refreshed and energized as if you had a good afternoon nap. You will be invigorated, have cognitive clarity, and be more productive throughout the day.

Additionally, **your body's "feel-good" chemicals will be released**, and you will enjoy a boost in your mood, a great sense of well-being, and peak mind and body energy levels.

3. Walking meditation

Technique: With this technique, you'll want a quiet and secluded area where you may walk very slowly. As you are walking, you should focus on your sensations of walking, your rhythm with each step as your feet touch the ground, the feeling of your body moving as you walk, and the subtlety of your body's physical balance.

Learning to stay focused while engaged in walking meditation requires the same level of self-patience as other methods for meditation.

Benefits: As with other forms of mindful meditation, a walking meditation assists you in remaining present while connected to your corporeal experiences. This technique helps you improve your capacity to focus while shutting out distractions. Pacing might be an example of walking meditation, minus the anxiety or rumination often associated with the action.

4. Single-tasking focus

Technique: Begin by selecting a single task on which to focus. Get rid of distractions by turning off your cell phone, closing nonessential browser tabs, closing your office door, etc. Focus your entire attention on that one task for a predetermined time period, such as twenty-five minutes (the Pomodoro method). If you experience a wandering mind, gently return to your task.

Benefits: When you focus on a single task for a sustained period of time, you are training your mind to be attentive. As you develop your ability to focus, you boost productivity and improve your efficiency. In short, if you want to get something important done, remove distractions and attack the task with a single-task attitude.

5. Additional Exercises

Engaging senses: Whether enjoying a meal or other activity enjoyed through your senses, take time to mindfully enjoy the experience using all your senses.

Observing thoughts: If you often have thoughts during meditation or other activities that interrupt your experiences, simply acknowledge the thought without judging it, let it pass, then go back to focusing on the previous activity.

Gratitude journaling: Gratitude can shift your attitude to help you live in the moment of each day with a more appreciative mindset. By keeping a journal about the things for which you are grateful each day, you cultivate a more meaningful and productive outlook.

Tips for success:

Start small, be consistent, be patient, and explore new techniques to find what resonates with you. Don't feel discouraged when your mind wanders; it's part of the learning process. Simply guide your focus back to the place it was before and continue.

There is much more about meditation available in volumes of books written over meditation's 2,600-year history. This book, *A Personal Success Tool Kit*, has spoon-fed you important basics that will help you build your own powerful success plan.

Here is my challenge to you: Master the art of mindfulness breathing meditation and mindfulness body scanning meditation over the next several weeks. As you practice mindfulness meditation, you will become more adept at controlling thoughts and actions in a natural, relaxed, and mentally alert state.

Regardless of the stress or anxiety you experience pursuing challenging goals, mindful meditation can help you level out the rough spots in your road to success!

Chapter Eight

SELF-HYPNOSIS FOR SUCCESS

Introduction to Self-Hypnosis

Have you ever driven home from work and not been able to remember anything about your drive? You weren't going crazy. You were simply in a state of hypnosis during your drive home. Your subconscious mind took over driving so you and the car could get home safely. It might seem a bit scary thinking about it, but being in a state of hypnosis happens to people everywhere every day.

When was the last time you experienced a good movie? Did you feel like you were right there with the hero or heroine, involved in the action and story? You were actually in a state of hypnosis.

Because your subconscious mind has no judgment, it cannot distinguish between fantasy and reality. Moviemakers are professionals in the art of creating hypnotic adventures. You are hypnotized by the music, sounds, acting, and scriptwriters.

Hypnosis is extensively used in modern medicine to cure illness, reduce pain, and improve healing. Many studies have proven that hypnosis prior to surgery reduces recovery time. In addition, hypnosis has proven effective in reducing the pain and length of discomfort with migraines. Self-hypnosis also offers many of these same benefits, except you are your own guide through the process of hypnosis

Self-hypnosis is safe, effective, and has no downside. The practice of self-hypnosis is simple enough that a young child can learn to do it. Self-hypnosis provides a way to attain a focused and relaxed cognitive state of mind. Then, while in that state, you are able to influence your feelings, behaviors, and thoughts to bring about desired positive changes.

Whether you are simply seeking the best self-help tools or you are an entrepreneur striving to achieve success, self-hypnosis will help you increase creativity, change behavior, achieve greater goals, manage time, and build a success-filled life.

Examples of how you might use self-hypnosis

- **Anxiety and stress control.** You will enjoy a feeling of relaxation while in the trance state that calms anxiety and stress better than medication.

- **Changing habits.** Unwanted habits can be

replaced with more desirable new habits, such as tobacco cessation, weight loss, or anger management.

- **Enhanced performance.** Professional athletes have long used self-hypnosis to program the perfect performance, improve confidence, and resilience.

- **Self-improvement.** Boost self-confidence, stop self-defeating behavior, or improve personal weaknesses to increase well-being and mental energy.

Primary characteristics of self-hypnosis

- **Self-direction.** Self-hypnosis is self-guided and personalized for your own goals and desires, versus going to a traditional or clinical hypnotist.

- **Practice-based.** Practice develops the skills to easily employ self-hypnosis and enjoy the benefits of self-improvement, goal achievement, and more.

- **Safe and effective.** Hypnosis is safe and proven effective. As you practice self-hypnosis, trust that it will work for you and have a plan for its use.

Note: If you struggle with serious psychological issues, I suggest you speak with a licensed counselor rather than trying to use self-hypnosis to heal yourself.

How Self-Hypnosis Works

Self-hypnosis is a trance-like, self-induced cognitive state in which you are deeply relaxed, focused, and totally aware. It bypasses the conscious mind and opens your subconscious mind to receive positive suggestion.

This hypnotic state allows your brain to generate alpha waves, which are linked with deep relaxation or a state of "creative flow." As you stay focused on your internal mental imagery or affirmations, you control your self-guided hypnotic trance state and tune out external stimuli.

The four-step process to self-hypnosis

1. Relax yourself and focus. Select a relaxing, quiet space where you will be free from interruptions. Get seated in a comfortable chair, recline on a couch, or lie on the floor. Using methods such as controlled breathing or progressive muscle relaxation, you will induce a deeply relaxed state as you guide yourself into self-hypnosis.

2. Visualization. As you become more deeply relaxed, you might choose to visualize a favorite, familiar place or scene. Visualize yourself achieving your desired goal or making the selected positive change, such as losing weight. You could visualize being thinner without craving snacks. See yourself accomplishing the thing you desire. Be positive in your thoughts and mental images. Eliminate negative words, actions, and images in your theater of the mind.

3. Make suggestions. Using positive affirmations, make post-hypnotic suggestions. Your suggestions should support your goals. Here are some examples of different types of positive affirmation:

- "I am feeling more calm, more peaceful, and more safe."

- "I'm sleeping more soundly and deeply each and every night."

- "I am breathing in relaxation and breathing out stress."

4. Back to awareness. As you begin to return to full awareness, do so gently and slowly. Count up from three down to one as you become more awake and aware. At one, open your eyes, you are fully awake, aware, and reoriented to your location.

Note: If you fall asleep during a self-hypnosis session, don't worry because you will awaken out of hypnosis. You won't get stuck in a self-hypnosis trance state.

How to Get Into Self-Hypnosis

I recommend the following two methods for use with self-hypnosis. You may also recall seeing these two methods in Chapter 7, CBT & Mindfulness. I have used both methods in clinical hypnotherapy sessions and in my own personal self-hypnosis sessions. I suggest using both methods several times to determine which method works best in your self-hypnosis sessions.

1. Controlled Breathing Method- A keystone of self-hypnosis and meditation.

Sit comfortably with your eyes closed. Breathe normally and become aware of the sensations of breathing as you breathe in and out. Focus on the feeling of air moving in and out of your lungs and the movement of your chest with each breath in and out. If your mind wanders (and it will), simply bring it back to focus on your breathing... gradually letting go of stress. Breathing in relaxation and breathing out stress.

Begin self-hypnosis with short 10-15 minute sessions and work up to longer sessions as you become more comfortable. Much like training a muscle, as you exercise your ability to focus, it will become stronger. You will soon tune out external sounds and interruptions.

As you become more relaxed and comfortable and feel ready to receive suggestions, allow planned mental images to fill your mind or use your internal voice to repeat positive affirmations.

As you become more comfortable with self-hypnosis, you might give yourself suggestions to go deeper and deeper into your trance state. When you feel totally relaxed and focused, you could add other pre-planned positive suggestions focused on making your desired positive changes.

When it's time to wake up from your trance state, count yourself out of trance, using a count of three, two, one, fully awake.

"Starting to awaken at 3, more awake now at 2, and at 1 wide awake. Fully awake."

Your body will feel refreshed, your mental energy will be elevated, and your motivation will be increased. Each time you practice getting into a trance state using controlled breathing, it will become easier to go rapidly into a trance state.

2. Body Scan Method- A versatile self-hypnosis and meditation method.

Lie comfortably on your back on the floor, bed, or couch. Or, if more comfortable, sit up in a chair with your back straight. Begin by closing your eyes and becoming aware of your feet and toes.

The method is to move your attention from one body part to the next as you move from toes to the top of your head or from head down to toes. For example, starting at your toes, scan your feet, then your ankles, shins, calves, knees, and so forth (scan both legs together rather than individually).

As you scan each body part, become aware of how it feels. Then, tell that body part to relax and scan the next body part. Upon arriving at the top of your head, all of your body should be very relaxed. In the beginning, your mind may wander (and it naturally will).

Guide your focus back to the body part being scanned, and continue until your body scan is complete. As you practice the body scan for relaxation and entry into self-hypnosis, you will become more proficient at achieving total relaxation more easily.

Through the **body scan method**, you tell each body part to "*Let go and relax*" as you focus on it. This technique helps to develop control of your body. In addition, as you identify tension in any body part, you develop the skill to let go of tension and relax that body part.

Begin self-hypnosis with short 10 to 15-minute sessions and work up to longer sessions as you become more comfortable. By the time you finish **scanning your entire body top to bottom or bottom**

to top, you should feel relaxed and ready to begin suggestions through visualization and affirmations.

Advanced tip: When you become more comfortable in self-hypnosis, give yourself the suggestion to "*go deeper and deeper and deeper*" into your hypno-trance. After doing this a few more times, and as you feel you are ready, add additional pre-planned suggestions regarding positive changes and achievements before waking up.

When it's time to wake up from your trance state, count yourself out of trance, using a count of three, two, one, fully awake.

"*Starting to awaken at 3, more awake now at 2, and at 1 wide awake. Fully awake.*"

Your body will feel refreshed, your mental energy will be elevated, and your motivation will be increased. You will come to feel as physically refreshed and energized as if you had a good afternoon nap. You will be invigorated, have cognitive clarity, and be more productive throughout the day.

Additionally, your body's "feel-good" chemicals will be released and you will enjoy a boost in your mood, a great sense of well-being, and peak mind and body energy levels.

A few final thoughts regarding your personal self-hypnosis plan

Planning your self-hypnosis sessions will help you become more effective. Being consistent in your practice and purposes will enable greater success.

Session Goal

Have a goal for each session. For example, the goal of your first four sessions may be to gain confidence in focusing and deep relaxation. As you progress, you might plan or pre-sketch mental images, mental videos, positive affirmations, or suggestions so you can suggest them to your subconscious mind using the theater of the mind technique while in a deeply relaxed trance.

Regular Practice

I suggest practicing 12–15 minutes per day, 3–5 days per week. This will develop your ability to create new neural pathways. Plus, each time you practice, your mental energy, ability to focus, and trance depth will increase. Keep at it and enjoy your experiences.

Feel Safe and Secure

You are 100 percent aware of yourself, your surroundings, and your level of relaxation (trance). Don't worry if you fall asleep during a session. Your body will awaken you automatically and remove you from your trance state. The good news is that you can't get stuck in a trance state with self-hypnosis.

Play Nice with Others

There are ten different success tools in this book that can be applied independently or used collectively. For example, visualization and positive affirmations can be used effectively within self-hypnosis to bring about positive changes. Both are independent tools and can be used without self-hypnosis for similar purposes.

Consider This

Using these ten personal success tools, you can set and achieve goals, improve time management, apply CBT or mindfulness principles, enhance spirituality, improve relationships, and expand your learning. And you can do each of these things independently or within self-hypnosis. Isn't that amazing?

Applications & Benefits of Self-Hypnosis

Self-hypnosis is exceptional for dealing with a broad spectrum of self-improvement issues. Although hypnosis as a whole can help over 360 known maladies, the focus here is limited to self-hypnosis's better-known applications and benefits such as the following list:

- **Pain Management:** Medical studies show that it is an effective tool for chronic pain. For example, self-hypnosis can reduce the length and pain of migraines. It is also a tool to reduce the levels of perceived pain before and after surgery.

- **Stress & Anxiety:** An excellent tool for reducing stress, anxiety, social anxiety, and more through deep relaxation, creating calmness and feelings of inner tranquility.

- **Increased Self-Confidence:** Self-confidence, self-esteem, self-image, and self-efficacy are all increased through positive self-hypnosis to boost your success.

- **Stop Limiting Self-Beliefs:** The effects of self-sabotage, self-limiting thoughts, and negative behaviors can be reversed to help you achieve greater success.

- **Reduce Fear:** Fear, timidity, social anxiety, or any emotion that causes an individual to withdraw from success can be improved dramatically via self-hypnosis.

- **Boost Motivation:** Most need an occasional kick in the rear to get motivated. It can more easily be done through self-hypnosis, so we help stay on track toward success.

- **Sleep Improvement:** Do you sleep well at night? Many need help to get a better night's sleep. Self-hypnosis is an excellent tool to fulfill this need for sleep.

- **Stop Unwanted/Bad Habits:** Want to stop smoking, chewing tobacco, lose weight, stop swearing, stop getting angry, or something else? This can help.

- **Stop Procrastination:** It doesn't do any good to have someone tell you to stop procrastinating, but self-hypnosis is you telling yourself in a way that does it!

- **Improve Focus:** Being focused on accomplishing our goals can sometimes get off track. If you need help with your ability to focus, self-hypnosis is the tool you need!

- **Achieve Goals:** Setting and achieving goals requires you to be consistent and committed. You can do it with consistent self-hypnosis about achieving your goals.

- **Achieve Success:** Do you really want to be successful? Self-hypnosis, coupled with the other nine tools in this book, will get you there. Make a plan. Stick to it. You will.

- **Performance Visualization:** Professional athletes, performers, and more use self-hypnosis to run mental videos of their performances and success. So can you!

These few examples of self-hypnosis applications may be useful in your personal quest for success. Make self-hypnosis a significant part of your weekly success plan.

Tip: Create an **anchor**, a *sensory trigger*, that will help you return to a positive state (emotional or confidence). It can be as simple as a word, phrase, gesture, or the touch of a finger on the back of your hand. This is done through self-hypnosis and can be a helpful hack in the pursuit of your goals.

Chapter Nine

SPIRITUALITY

The Prerequisite to Success

You may be wondering, "*How is spirituality a personal success tool?*" Whether or not you are Christian, Jewish, Buddhist, Muslim, atheist, agnostic, or any other religion of the world, we all have **two things in common**. First, we all have **a physical body** or outer self. Second, we all have **a spirit** or inner self.

Additionally, as human beings, we have similar needs, passions, and desires. Our lives are focused, even preconditioned to fulfill our needs, such as:

Survival: food, shelter, safety, work**Family:** generations of man, woman, and offspring**Emotion:** happiness, sadness, love, hate**Dreams:** hope, disappointment, trust, success**Faith:** belief in a greater power than ourselves or in ourselves

Here is the point

Since the time of Adam and Eve, the men and women who became the leaders and spiritual guides for their tribes embodied integrity, service to others, compassion, and spiritual strength for their society to follow. You likewise can **become a leader within your spheres of influence.**

Since time began, beloved kings, queens, prosperous merchants, philosophers, and scholars have applied *inner self* skills to enrich themselves. These noble leaders were highly esteemed because of their kindness, integrity, charity, and leadership. **They influenced entire civilizations for the better** without using guile, intrigue, or force. Subsequently, their fame spread far and wide across the known world.

Dr. Albert Schweitzer (1875–1965) was one such man. He was a Renaissance man who was ahead of his time. He was a physician, humanitarian, philosopher, and theologian. Dr. Schweitzer dedicated years of his life to humanitarian medical efforts in the heart of Africa. In 1952, he received the Nobel Peace Prize along with $33,000, which he used to help fund his work in Africa.

When asked why he had given so many years of his life to medical service in Africa, Dr. Schweitzer simply said, **"The purpose of human life is to serve and to show compassion and the will to help others."**

This statement beautifully sums up one of the most relevant inner-self key principles shared in this chapter. To become a success in life, you must be willing to exchange a modicum of personal gratification for a measure of happiness!"

Happiness is created by giving kind service to anyone you meet who is in need of help. This is the proven method for finding true happiness, which has been taught to men and women since time began. And as a physician, it was a powerful principle in Albert Schweitzer's life to serve the sick and poverty-ridden villages in Africa.

Among his inner circle of associates, Albert observed that **success** and **happiness** were somehow connected. As a philosopher and deep thinker, he wanted to understand how it was that his friends and associates were both successful and happy.

Albert was fascinated by the fact that these men were humanitarians like himself. They all gave of their money and time generously to help orphans, widows, the sick, and the poor.

Whenever Albert's inner circle discussed the topic, differing philosophical viewpoints emerged regarding the connection between **success** and **happiness**. A few put forth ideas that success was life's aim and that a person found happiness through marriage, hobbies, or other pursuits.

Some contended that success came first and created its own state of happiness. Others totally separated the two and suggested that neither success nor happiness had the slightest connection with the other. Albert's initial concept of the connection between success and happiness met with rejection.

Eventually, Albert persuaded this group of associates to accept his unusual idea. This was a radical new philosophy for its day. As Dr. Schweitzer put it, "*success is not the key to happiness! Happiness is the key to success!*

Two **powerful truths** shared by Dr. Albert Schweitzer. The **first truth** is that **happiness is the prerequisite to success**! Happiness flows into our soul, our **inner-self**, with every nonjudgmental act of kindness and service we perform for others.

Happiness comes when we stop thinking about ourselves and think instead about helping other people. This action fulfills our deeper emotional and physiological needs that lead to even greater feelings of happiness. "*Service to others boosts mental energy and positively stimulates neurotransmitters that flood the body with feel-good chemicals.*"

The **second truth** is that **the more service you give, the happier your life becomes!** You are literally empowered by God, the universe, or greater power to achieve ever more daunting goals in your life.

You become enabled to handle life's daunting challenges and complete difficult tasks with ease. **You are blessed with success through service.** Additionally, you find favor in the eyes of people around you when you serve others. You become elevated as "*One whom others trust and look to for guidance and wisdom.*"

Serving others with kindness is one of life's rarest and most needed activities! As the giver of much-needed help, your life will become filled with happiness. This is not a cheap imitation of happiness. Rather, this is **true happiness that energizes your heart, soul, hopes, and dreams**. A great prophet who lived a few hundred years before the time of Jesus Christ once stated: "***When you are in the service of your fellow beings, you are only in the service of your God.***"   King Benjamin

This is absolutely true!

Set these two goals today

Don't procrastinate or forget. Your ultimate success in whatever endeavor you choose depends upon your service to others and the happiness this philosophy will add to your life.

1. Exchange selfishness for nonjudgmental service to others.

Open your heart to the joy of boosting hope, drying tears, taking away fear, and doing what you can to improve the quality of life for anyone who may be in need. Service to others will boost your mental energy, **engage your brain's neurotransmitters** to release feel-good brain chemicals, and magnify your success.

2. Discover happiness through everything you do in life.

Strive to become the person others look to for leadership and understanding. As you seek happiness, your creativity, self-esteem, and self-confidence will grow exponentially. **Happiness is life's paramount achievement!**

Self-Evaluations

"Wherever you may be in the musical scale of life, there is always a higher note you can aspire to sing." Robert D. Hutchings

Developing a more positive inner-self is a consistent daily activity that is coupled with successfully achieving your goals. The following three self-evaluations have been designed to help expand your self-awareness. Please take extra time to complete both evaluations.

Self-Evaluation 1

There are two side-by-side lists. Read the first word in List 1 then read the first word in List 2. There are no right or wrong answers. Use a pencil to circle the trait you feel most accurately represents how you see or feel about your inner-self (spiritual self). Continue the process down the lists of 25 traits. You may find it preferable to write your answers in a notebook rather than in the book.

There is no such thing as a perfect score. Every human being has spiritual traits from both lists, regardless of religion or cultural backgrounds. **You know yourself intimately.** Be honest with yourself. Select the word the most closely reflects how you see or feel about your inner-self.

Self-Evaluation 1: How do you perceive your inner-self?

List #1   **List #2**

List #1	List #2
_____ Loving	_____ Numb
_____ Kind	_____ Pleasant
_____ Respectful	_____ Reserved
_____ Serving	_____ Comfortable
_____ Hopeful	_____ Resigned
_____ Fearless	_____ Concerned
_____ Truthful	_____ Cunning
_____ Faithful	_____ Fickle
_____ Good	_____ Decadent

_____	Happy	_____	Fateful
_____	Godly	_____	Worldly
_____	Charitable	_____	Critical
_____	Prayerful	_____	Flattering
_____	Believing	_____	Dubious
_____	Trusting	_____	Devious
_____	Virtuous	_____	Errant
_____	Honest	_____	Faux
_____	Integrity	_____	Ruthless
_____	Moral	_____	Erudite
_____	Humble	_____	Pompous
_____	Grateful	_____	Ungracious
_____	Spiritual	_____	Atheistic
_____	Disciple	_____	Apostate
_____	Inspired	_____	Stagnation

Score yourself.

1. Add +1 point for each trait you select from List 1.

2. Subtract -1 point for each trait you select from List 2.

3. What percentage is from List #1? What percentage is from List #2?

4. Review this list of inner traits. Write them down in a notebook.

5. Now, create a list of the traits you want to change with their corresponding new traits.

6. Set a goal for yourself to change less desirable traits for more positive inner traits.

How did you do? Any personal traits you care to change or improve? Write down the inner-self traits you desire to acquire, change, or eliminate. Use visualization, positive affirmations, and self-hypnosis to help you make the desired changes.

Developing strong, positive, inner-self traits is a powerful tool to help you gain greater happiness and you prepare yourself to shoulder the greater success that will soon be flowing unto you.

How Do Others Perceive You?

A recent research study at Cornell University uncovered that many social media profiles get ranked higher for self-esteem by other users than by profile owners themselves. It was determined that most people see themselves in a more negative light than how others actually view them.

Biases that color self-image

The following biases can skew your assessment of personal accomplishments, behavior, and success.

- **Internal vs. external perspective bias** Based on your internal feelings and thoughts, you may generate a negative self-judgment. However, people will develop their impressions of you based on your external behavior and traits they perceive about you. Thus, your internal assessment is always dissimilar from the observer's perception.

- **Differences in personality bias** Some view themselves as being more positive, more motivated, and more open to new experiences than others may view them. This bias can lead to problems when difficulties arise.

- **Looking-glass self-bias** You construct your "*self-concept*" based upon how you imagine other people perceive you. This bias results in error.

- **Influence of culture bias** Your internal cultural influence can play a strong role in how you see yourself and in how others perceive you. However, most studies confirm that the differences in your self-assessment and the observations of others remain constant across cultures.

- **Self-serving outlook bias** Individuals who tend to have inflated feelings of self-worth and oversized egos develop distorted internal assessments. This can expand the gap between this person's self-concept and the observed traits of other people.

- **Motivational prejudice bias** Your skills and abilities may be embellished due to "*self-motivation*" to enhance your self-value. People tend to be more objective in perceiving your traits since theirs is not a self-interest-based observation.

- **Frames of reference bias** You filter self-assessment through biases such as emotion, personal experience, or attitudes. Additionally, "*projection*" is a well-known psychological phenomenon in which one attributes their own personal traits to the personal traits of another.

Self-Evaluation 2: How Do Others Perceive You?

Self-Evaluation 2 helps you think of the personal traits others may use to describe you. Allow some some extra time to complete this self-evaluation. As you select the traits you think others might use to describe you, be aware of the self-image biases previously described.

Instructions:

1. Select all traits from either column you feel other people may use to describe you and your outward behavior.

2. Mark the trait and create a list in a notebook

for later review.

3. Remember, there are no right or wrong answers-be honest with yourself.

4. If you think of other words not on the list, write them in your notebook under self-evaluation 2. Use this list to get started with your own in-depth self evaluation. Add any other traits that come to mind- good or bad. Try to get a clear picture of areas you feel may need some change or improvement. You know yourself best.

Self Evaluation 2: How Do Others Perceive You?

_____	Smart	_____	Wise
_____	Obedient	_____	Fearful
_____	Grateful	_____	Humble
_____	Honest	_____	Empathetic
_____	Peaceable	_____	Listener
_____	Leader	_____	Genuine
_____	Patient	_____	Prideful
_____	Kind	_____	Hateful
_____	Depressed	_____	Envious
_____	Charitable	_____	Strong
_____	Generous	_____	Weak
_____	Giving	_____	Teacher
_____	Envious	_____	Follower
_____	Angry	_____	Prayerful

_____	Happy	_____	Thoughtful
_____	Valuable	_____	Confident
_____	Trustworthy	_____	Passive
_____	Helpful	_____	Decisive
_____	Organized	_____	Creative
_____	Conceited	_____	Productive
_____	Stingy	_____	Practical
_____	Deceitful	_____	Integrity
_____	Embellisher	_____	Counselor

Now, write down all the personality traits you selected in your notebook. Look over the list. Are they positive? Not so positive? What traits would you improve on the list? Remember, these are traits you feel others might use to describe your outward behavior.

With these two self-evaluation exercises, you should now be aware of who you think you are spiritually (Self-Evaluation 1) and the personality traits others may see in you outwardly and use to describe you (Self-Evaluation 2).

Self Evaluation 3: What Positive Traits Are You Missing?

Make a list of real individuals you know or with whom you associate who exhibit positive, charismatic personality traits—both observed and perceived by you. As you consider each individual, ask yourself these questions:

What are the personality traits this person possesses that makes them magnetic? Do I have these traits? Can I develop these traits if I do not have them? Think of people you know who:

- Are charismatic
- Are leaders
- Have integrity
- Are top performers
- People who keep going when things get tough
- People who never give up.
- People who always seem to beat the odds to become even more successful.

Using the your new skills of *visualization, positive affirmation, CBT-mindfulness, and self-hypnosis*, you can acquire, improve, or eliminate inner-self and external traits that are success limiters. Remember, do not allow biases to influence your self-belief in who you are, in who you think you are, or in who you are becoming.

Become the Real Deal

The fact is that society will judge you based upon whatever it perceives about you. You could pretend to have positive personality traits and "**get by**" socially. However, sooner or later, others would learn that you were just a phony. Sooner or later you would be humiliated and swept into the gutter of life. So, don't do it! **Do not pretend to be someone you are not. Do not take the lazy shortcut to temporary success!**

Develop your own, true, desirable personality traits that people admire, respect, and follow. Become a quality leader among your peers, in your community, on the job, or in your chosen profession. Nothing is holding you back. You now have the most powerful personal success tools at your fingertips, designed to boost you toward success and the achievement of amazing goals.

With these proven success tools as your secret weapons, you now have **the secrets to unstoppable accomplishment and success!**

Tip: Use time management methods, SMART goal-setting methods, visualization, positive affirmations, CBT-mindfulness, self-hypnosis, and self-evaluation skills to improve your inward and outward personality success traits.

Chapter Ten

RELATIONSHIPS

The Benefits of Quality Relationships

Quality relationships have a dynamic, direct, and indirect influence upon personal success! Let me repeat that. The quality of your relationships have a dynamic, direct and indirect influence upon your personal success!

According to research, the positive benefits derived from engaging in active social relationships can include encouragement when it's needed, motivation to achieve BHAGs (Big Hairy Audacious Goals), and feelings of well-being. Those who seek out and develop strong social relationships are happier, have better emotional health, are better motivated, and experience less stress when challenges arise.

Positive social and romantic relationships are **the best predictors** of a person's happiness and success in life. Positive relationships and social connections with others outweighs genetics, income, or intellect as **a means test for success**. Your relationships are not inconsequential. They are your personal support system that nurtures and boosts your efforts. Let's examine a few of the direct and indirect benefits more in depth.

Direct benefits of positive social relationships

- **Accountability and encouragement:** Friends and associates will help you remain focused on achieving goals, provide accountability, and cheer you on in your quest to achieve greater goals. This social support is *psychological capital*. It's what keeps you on track with accomplishing goals, boosts your self-confidence, and increases mental energy.

- **New opportunities:** The use of social networking for personal and business purposes is a potent success tool. Building relationships of trust cultivates **strong bonds of friendship**. Actively engaging in established social networking groups and civic organizations is a source of new relationships that may also become a source for new opportunities.

- **Differing perceptions:** Most social and civic organizations include members from diverse backgrounds. Relationships with a variety of people who have different backgrounds can often generate innovative approaches that can help you achieve your most tenacious goals. Your social relationships may also include individuals with real-life experience who can help you solve difficult challenges you may encounter in pursuit of your goals.

- **Important feedback:** Relationships of trust are developed as you work together in civic organizations, social networking groups, work groups, and church organizations. These relationships offer **a safe environment** for positive feedback and individual growth. Honest feedback is an incredibly positive benefit for any individual focused on personal improvement.

Indirect benefits of positive social relationships

- **Physical and emotional benefits:** Enjoying positive social relationships can benefit overall health by **reducing depression and anxiety**. You will also enjoy feelings of belonging, a sense of well-being, improved confidence, reduced stress, and increased mental energy.

- **Enhanced spirit:** Support from others during difficult times can help you cope more easily. You can rebound from difficulties and setbacks quickly and feel more empowered to keep trying with support from those around you.

- **Greater sense of self:** If you experience negative thoughts or feelings about yourself, your social relationships can help you improve your self-esteem and self-confidence. Through relationships of trust, your success can become an expectation rather than simply a dream.

Your spheres of influence

Your positive relationships include family, friends, social connections, romantic partners, and work-related associations. We refer to these categories as "spheres of influence." **Every sphere of influence is essential to your personal success.** Relationships must be based upon the foundation of honesty, trust, respect, and service to others.

Bear in mind that these are personal, intimate, sacred, and trusted personal connections. For this reason, I do not refer to relationships in terms of being success tools. Rather (and this is a crucial step), **seek out and establish positive social relationships.** Your personal spheres of influence will be your most valuable support team and they will amplify your success beyond your own abilities.

To further set the picture, relationships are not to be "used" inappropriately in this process. **Be genuine,**

real, and honest in every relationship. There is enormous power in establishing and cultivating positive social relationships.

Magic happens when generosity, kindness, help, respect, and encouragement are shared socially. You will begin to experience upward growth into exciting new levels of opportunities and success-mindedness.

How Relationships Expand Mental Energy

Relationships and social connections are renewable sources of mental energy. **Your mental energy becomes like a storage depot.** The demands of daily living may run your reserves dry. However, intimate relationships can fill up your reserves quite efficiently by eliminating the stress that depletes them.

When you share your inner self with a loved one, the bonding hormone *oxytocin* is released. This hormone combats "anxiety-producing" cortisol to reduce stress and anxiety. A study conducted in 2023 found that those who enjoyed supportive relationships during periods of high stress experienced **a 25 percent reduction in mental fatigue**.

Having a friend or partner with whom you can vent your frustrations not only feels good, but also frees up mental energy to enhance your problem-solving abilities. Such a relationship also **increases cognitive activity**, expands neural pathways, and increases focus and creativity. You both benefit from this bond of friendship.

Relationships are dynamic mechanisms

Here are seven dynamic relationships that include a brief description and suggestions for building better relationships within the category. As mechanisms for building personal success, positive relationships in all categories is an essential asset. Few soldiers of fortune ever reach nirvana without positive relationships.

1. Social Associates

- Low-stakes interactions requiring little emotional investment.

- Attend regularly; requires light interaction; follow-up using text messages.

- Build rapport; give sincere compliments; offer resources without over-commitment.

- Locate groups using apps (i.e., Meetup); expand connections with at least one new person after meeting them the first time at an event.

2. Friends

- Spend time together; share experiences; have fun; play; reduce stress.

- Plan regular time together; check-ins for

coffee or lunch; be consistent.

- Listen actively; reciprocate time to speak; offer support if requested.

- Plan shared time; participate in common activities; be accessible to play.

3. Romantic Relationships (Not Married)

- Build intimacy; long-term fulfillment.

- Open communication; set boundaries; discuss needs; use "I" statements.

- Create fun rituals; weekly dates; thoughtfulness; be on time; bring gifts.

- Do couples activities; build trust; apologize if needed; be nonjudgmental.

4. Spouses

- Provide lifelong stability; provide emotional security; life planning.

- Prioritize relationship; morning check-ins; stay aligned in work-life needs.

- Actively listen; allow reciprocity; give more than receive; put spouse first.

- Divide responsibilities; work together for

family; loyalty to spouse.

- Give love freely, not as a reward; be honest about feelings; address issues.

5. Work Associates

- Professional; collaborative; problem-solving; skill-sharing.

- Build reciprocity; help with work projects; develop common interests.

- Lunch chats; team feedback; brainstorm problem solutions; reduce isolation.

- Join professional groups; become allies with other associates; service.

6. Church Groups

- Spiritual support; shared values; promote peace and love.

- Participate actively; increase understanding; charitable giving; service.

- Volunteer for service; offer prayers; learn beliefs; grow in understanding.

- Fellowship with others; meet regular members; join Bible discussion groups.

7. School Groups (Study Group/Alumni)

- Learning; intellectual exchanges; skills.

- Organize group; join current groups; join in virtual lessons; active study.

- Post-graduate connections; use school apps; add yourself to mailing lists.

- Contribute to alumni fund; support alumni activities; attend activities.

If you were in the military, you may want to join the American Legion, Veterans of Foreign Wars (VFW), or Disabled American Veterans (DAV). **These are simply starting points.** Start developing your own strategy for developing a personalized sphere of influence.

Mechanisms for Boosting Success

We previously discussed relationships in general terms. Now, let's put a fine point on "how" building quality relationships are a mechanism for boosting your success and mental energy.

1. Mechanisms That Boost Success

- **Accountability and Support:** High-quality relationships deliver encouragement and productive feedback that can turn unclear ambitions into executable plans. For example, a good friend could hold you responsible to achieve a fitness goal. Accountability can increase success by 65 percent, according to a Dominican University study. In comparison, a low-quality friend is not interested in your priority of achieving this personal goal and might even criticize you if you fail.

- **Opportunity Development:** High-quality associations and relationships can become bridges to helpful new resources. Consider a professional situation in which a mentor with whom you have bonded might recommend you for an open position. In comparison, a shallow connection would rarely go that extra mile to help you get a better job. According to a 2023 LinkedIn report, 70 percent of professionals give credit for their career advancements to high-quality connections and relationships.

- **Building Resilience:** High-quality relationships provide empathy and the help to bounce back during failures. Their continuing efforts help you achieve long-term success. Successful entrepreneurs credit supportive relationships and partners for their perseverance throughout the startup process.

2. Mechanisms That Expand Mental Energy

- **Stress Reduction:** High-quality relationships share problems and failures. They allow you to offload discouragement and emotional weight without judgment. This conserves mental energy and recharges cognitive strength. A Yale neuroimaging study displayed evidence that empathetic conversations provide real benefits. They activate cognitive reward centers, improve focus, and reduce mental fatigue. In comparison, low-quality connections drain mental energy and do nothing to replace it.

- **Cognitive Stimulation:** High-quality connections interact with creative ideas, innovative problem-solving suggestions, and mental energy-boosting encouragement. For example, a friend or spouse offers insightful observations that spawn discussion about how to solve difficulties affecting goal achievement. Low-quality connections would not interact with such enthusiasm to help you overcome obstacles to success.

- **Emotional Vitality:** High-quality relationships are based on feelings of belonging, which boost dopamine and endorphins. Based on positive psychology research, this creates "psychological capital" such as hope, efficacy, and increased levels of mental energy.

Low-quality connections drain psychological capital.

Conclusion

"Creating a life you love starts with mindset, resilience, and a heart for helping others. Small choices and daily habits build big futures." Zig Ziglar

Imagine two different professionals managing career setbacks. The first has high-quality relationships: a spouse who is supportive and friends who listen, encourage, and motivate. These relationships stimulate a quick recovery, boost mental energy, and embolden a quick turnaround to begin a new adventure.

The second professional is bitter, has few quality connections, and is toxic toward the career setback. Feeling depressed, heavy stress sets in, stalls progress, and drains mental energy. There is no one to support, encourage, listen, or motivate. Recovery seems impossible, and the idea of pivoting to a new venture never comes.

What is the difference? High-quality relationships and associations! Such relationships directly fuel mental energy, quality of life, and success. Essentially, **high-quality relationships are the success multiplier.** They energize you mentally and biologically. They empower you psychologically. Socially, they propel you upward into the jet stream of success.

In order to cultivate high-quality relationships, **you must focus on authenticity**, gratitude, mutual concern for well-being, and mutual growth. Quality requires consistent, focused attention and effort.

Tip: Choose quality associations and friendships over quantity of connections or low-value associations.

Chapter Eleven

LEARNING

The Benefits of Lifetime Learning

A lifetime of learning delivers far more exciting benefits than simply mining for success every day. Among these benefits are very real psychological, cognitive, and physical well-being. Understanding the true benefits of learning and how learning accelerates success while increasing mental energy is the underpinning of this chapter.

"When you change your thinking, you change your actions; when you change your action, you change your future." Zig Ziglar

Learning is one of the most powerful tools for increasing psychological and physical abilities to achieve impressive goals. It comes in all different shapes and sizes. Whether or not you have an advanced degree is not the point. The point is that you engage in classes, hobbies, reading, or learning by doing something new. It means staying mentally active.

Learning is the personal success tool that can deliver the greatest return for your time invested. Let's begin by reviewing eight beneficial areas where a lifetime of learning will help you in your quest for success.

Eight key benefits obtained by prioritizing learning as a lifetime goal.

1. Cognitive Health

Stimulating mental activity keeps your brain functioning in top condition. If you are young, this should be your natural state of mind. Regardless of age, mental activity lowers your risk of neurodegenerative disorders like dementia and Alzheimer's disease. Learning expands your neural pathways (neuroplasticity) to improve mental energy, and functions like attention, problem-solving, mental sharpness, and memory.

2. Emotional and Mental Well-Being

As you develop new skills and master new topics, your sense of accomplishment will soar. You will also enjoy an enormous lift to your self-confidence, self-esteem, and personal motivation. Learning can provide relief from boredom, depression, and stress, and reduce anxiety. It can also renew your sense of purpose, especially after life-changing challenges.

3. Physical Well-Being

Learning new physical activities involving physical movement can enhance overall physical health and well-being. Activities such as yoga, weight lifting, dancing, bowling, and even gardening involve learning new skills. Gaining competencies takes time and practice, which adds to overall cognitive maintenance.

4. Flexibility and Adaptability

Learning new skills, especially digital skills, helps you stay connected in the rapidly changing technical world. With the world engaging in faster, more secure technology, keeping up with needed technical skills can help you expand your business presence and connections, as well as personal social skills.

5. Neural Stimulation

Your brain, like a muscle, needs regular exercise to stay healthy and strong. **Learning stimulates your brain**, expands neural pathways, and can result in feel-good chemicals flooding your brain as a bonus.

6. Increased Efficiency

As you learn, your body produces *myelin*. This chemical **creates protective sheaths around nerve fibers** that increase communication speed and efficiency among neurons. This faster processing speed instantly creates greater cognitive alertness and vitality.

7. Cognitive Reserve

Over time, **consistent learning builds a "cognitive reserve"** that gives the brain the ability to resist disease or damage. An expanded reserve leads to your brain being able to deliver better function for longer periods when challenged with age-related illness. This also leads to greater mental energy.

8. Fights Mental Stagnation

Without the enhancement of learning, your cognitive functions will slow down, leading to a state of mental fog. **Learning keeps your brain actively engaged.** Learning is a crucial channel for improving personal productivity and expanding valuable mental energy.

There is an ancient Chinese proverb that says, *"Learning is a treasure that will follow its owner everywhere."*

How Learning Is a Tool for Success

Benjamin Franklin once commented that ***"Growth is essential for improvement and success,"*** meaning that the impact of learning rests in its ability to drive your personal and professional growth and success.

The purpose of learning is not simply to gain new knowledge and ideas. **It is about gaining the knowledge needed in order to take action which is the mechanism that drives success!**

Thus, learning is connected to success **through the mechanism of action**. Without action, learning alone cannot fulfill your dreams and goals. You must always connect learning to action in order to achieve your BHAGs in life.

Here is an example: After attending a class to learn about gardening, you decide to put what you learned into action. You carefully prepare your ground with a tiller to break up and aerate the soil, add some organic nutrients, and prepare rows of soil in which to plant your seeds. You plant carrots, tomatoes, lettuce, onions, corn, and squash according to recommended seed depths and spacing.

However, there is much more work to be done to grow a successful garden. Left unattended, the garden would not survive. You must regularly provide the seeds and young plants with sufficient water, pull the weeds, manage insect attacks, trap plant-eating rodents, and fence out unwanted critters to protect your crops.

Are you done yet? No, there is still more to do. You must actively care for each and every plant in your garden until it is time to harvest your vegetables. Finally, your garden is producing delicious vegetables, and you can harvest the fruits of your labor. Success is realized!

Learning is a tool for success.

As the gardener, you were motivated to take action and plant the garden by what you learned in the class. If you had attended the gardening class but did nothing with what you learned, the ground would be left barren. This same principle applies to achieving any success in life. Learning is a tool for achieving greater success.

Regardless of any prior education or degree, if you ignore lifelong learning, your success will be comparable to that of the barren garden. Any learning already received would be wasted. Your motivation dried up. Success would simply be a a long forgotten dream.

In contrast, when you learn something new and exciting, get motivated by your new knowledge, and take positive action, you are **personally and professionally rewarded with success**.

The Success Matrix

Learning provides knowledge that boosts **Motivation** which results in taking **Action** to **Complete** a goal. The result is **SUCCESS**!

The Success Matrix formula:

L/M + A/C = S
L = Learning, M = Motivation, A = Action, C = Completion, S = Success

This is **A Personal Success Tool Kit's Success Matrix.** This is a real-life, simplified formula for achieving everything you desire in life. Put it to the test. It works! In fact, if you fail at anything you strive to achieve using this formula, simply troubleshoot the weakest link in the chain which is the human factor.

Conclusion

In conclusion, let's review how learning acts as a tool for personal and professional success. Seeking new learning opportunities expands your mindset to seize on exciting new opportunities and to purposefully take action.

Remember that **action is the mechanism that connects learning to success**. Action is the beginning and ending of every successful achievement. Make the **Success Matrix** an active part of your success planning.

Seven ways learning acts as a tool for personal and professional success:

1. Cultivate a Growth Mindset

Learning helps build a growth mindset and belief in your own capabilities to succeed in everything you do.

2. Enhance Resilience and Adaptability

Learning equips you to stay relevant in a rapidly changing world with shifting demands.

3. Boost Confidence and Self-Efficacy

Learning a new software program, a new language, or new skills boosts self-esteem and self-confidence.

4. Increase Critical Thinking and Problem-Solving

Learning stimulates curiosity, creativity, critical thinking, and problem-solving capacities.

5. Unlock Exciting Opportunities

Learning via self-directed personal development books, audio and video programs can improve income and career advancement.

6. Expand Personal Development

Learning opens doors to a better understanding of yourself and your world. Exploring interests will enrich the quality of your life.

7. Strengthen Relationships and Social Connections

Learning in social settings, such as workshops or through online communities, develops communication skills.

Thirteen Ideas for Continuous Learning and Boosting Mental Energy:

- Listen to audiobooks, podcasts, interviews
- Watch online videos regarding topics of interest
- Read books, articles, online content
- Take online classes to explore interesting topics
- Participate in live workshops and skill training
- Take up a new hobby to challenge your mind
- Learn to play a new instrument
- Learn to speak a new language
- Write a book about a new topic
- Master a karate or kung fu class
- Engage in brain games such as Sudoku
- Use online brain puzzle apps
- Complete challenging crossword puzzles

Tip: Always include the **Success Matrix** in your plans to achieve BHAGs.

Chapter Twelve

UNPACKING YOUR SUCCESS TOOLS
Getting Started

This chapter brings together the entirety of *A Personal Success Tool Kit*. Whether you choose to include ten success tools in your weekly schedule or a few select tools is up to you. As you begin to unpack your tool kit, please take adequate time to set up each tool as suggested. This process is a hands-on experience for using your tools. Be sure to have a notebook and a couple of pens handy before you begin.

Unpacking Your Tools

Let's get started. I suggest keeping all your work and notes in one notebook. Write down the tool name, suggested actions to take, descriptions, and ideas that occur during the process. You may want to refer back to your notes in order to integrate tools into personal or professional projects.

1. Goal Setting

A PERSONAL SUCCESS TOOL KIT

This is one of the key elements of success. You may already have several goals upon which you are presently working. Or you may just be getting started with setting goals. Whatever your situation, I recommend starting with the S.M.A.R.T. method for setting and/or expanding personal and professional goals.

Set Two New Goals. Write out your new goals using the S.M.A.R.T. method.

- Goal #1:

- Goal #2:

2. Time Management

Success can be positively or negatively impacted based on your time management skills. Good time management puts you in control of productivity. The brain gets flooded with feel-good chemicals that boost mood while eliminating stress and feelings of overwhelm. This boosts mental energy, goal achievement, and success. I suggest the Pomodoro technique for time-consuming tasks such as computer work.

Select a Time Management Method. Write down the details regarding your chosen time management method and how you plan to deploy it.

- Describe the time management method you

will use daily

3. Visualization

Visualization is the act of creating mental images within your imagination in order to simulate scenarios, experiences, and events. Visualization is a cognitive dry run during which emotions, thoughts, and behaviors are rehearsed, and real-life neural pathways are activated. Visualization can boost personal and professional performance to significantly drive a successful outcome.

Visualize a Goal. Select one of your new goals and describe the details to be used in the goal visualization session.

- Describe how you will visualize Goals #1 and #2 as detailed as possible.

4. Positive Affirmations

Positive affirmations employ neuroplasticity to rewire the brain. They work deep down in the subconscious mind and can help to develop automatic new behavior. Affirmations must always align with your values and goals. Always use *present-tense-active* language when writing your positive affirmations.

Read affirmations out loud frequently, repetitively, and consistently. For example, read them each morning at breakfast or every evening at bedtime. Affirmations are powerful tools for inner change.

Write a positive affirmation for each one of your new goals using present-tense active language.

- (a) Describe how your positive affirmations will change or improve desired behavior; (b) decide how many times per day you will read them out loud; and (c) when you will repeat them out loud.

- Create affirmations for Goal#1 and #2 as detailed as possible.

5. Cognitive Behavioral Therapy (CBT)

CBT provides an organized means to recognize and alter negative thoughts, feelings, and behaviors. It offers useful approaches to manage stress and emotions and resolve daily life problems. It gives invaluable strategies to advance feelings of well-being, improve mood, increase motivation, and stay focused on long-term success.

Review CBT (Chapter 7). Use CBT to query those thoughts and select a more positive perspective—**reframe negative thoughts or feelings**. Keep in mind goals #1 and #2 and watch for negative self-talk to goal achievement.

6. Mindfulness and Mindfulness Meditation

Mindfulness works by focusing on the current moment and accepting thoughts or feelings without judgment to decrease stress levels. The goal of mindfulness is to change your relationship with thoughts, versus changing the thought (CBT works to change the thought).

Review Mindfulness (Chapter 7). Use Mindfulness to change thoughts and select a more positive thinking—**reframe negative thoughts or feelings**. Keep in mind goals #1 and #2 and watch for negative self-talk during goal achievement.

Practice Mindfulness Meditation's Focused Breathing Technique. Sit comfortably with eyes closed. Breathe normally and become aware of the sensations of breathing as you breathe in and out. Focus on the feeling of air moving in and out of your lungs and the movement of your chest with each breath in and out.

In the beginning, your mind will naturally wander. Gently guide your mind back to focusing on breathing. Limit sessions to 10 or 15 minutes. Keep in mind goals #1 and #2 and watch for stress during goal achievement.

7. Self-Hypnosis

Self-hypnosis is safe, effective, and has no downside. The practice of self-hypnosis is simple to learn.

Through self-hypnosis, you can attain a focused and relaxed cognitive state of mind, and while in that relaxed state, be able to influence change to bring about desirable positive changes.

It can help reduce or eliminate stress, anxiety, lack of self-confidence, and more. Self-hypnosis can increase your creativity, change behaviors, achieve BHAGs, better manage time, and build a more robust and success-filled life.

Use the Body Scan method to induce self-hypnosis. Begin with 15-minute sessions and lengthen sessions as you become more comfortable. When you complete the body scan, you should feel relaxed. It's at this point that you are ready to give yourself positive suggestions or visualize a goal. Use self-hypnosis to help achieve goals #1 and #2 and manage stress, anxiety, or fear during during goal achievement process.

8. Spirituality

Spirituality is about becoming the best person you can become. It focuses upon several key principles. **"The purpose of human life is to serve and to show compassion and the will to help others,"** and **"Success is not the key to happiness! Happiness is the key to success!**

Thus, we see that service to others boosts happiness, and both are key elements to success. Spirituality also directs our attention to evaluating ourselves, then striving to improve our characteristics to become more charismatic and integrity-based individuals.

Make a list of positive character traits you wish to acquire (eliminate). Create a list of desirable character traits you would like to include within yourself. Use self-hypnosis coupled with affirmations and visualization to develop or change character traits.

- Begin with only one trait at a time. Only move to a new one when you feel successful in integrating the first character trait (or eliminating your first unwanted trait). Work on new traits every 30 days.

9. Relationships

Positive relationships are the best predictors of a person's happiness and success in life. Positive social connections are not about genetics, income, or intellect, per se. Quality relationships have positive consequences for long-term success.

They become your personal and professional support system. They mitigate failure when challenges come along. They boost confidence to achieve greater goals, and they can provide positive health benefits such as stress reduction.

Make a list of your top 20–30 quality relationships. These may include your spouse, significant other, family members, close friends, and long-time work buddies. Create a second list of 20–30 solid social connections with whom you associate that could become better quality.

Review your list of relations. Review your *quality relationships* list to identify those who would be willing to help you if some catastrophe struck in your life.

- Also, review your *social connections list* to identify individuals that could become better quality or top-quality relationships. Create an action plan to assess the desires of your targeted contacts and to expand those relationships accordingly.

10. Learning

Learning is a powerful tool that increases your psychological and physical abilities to achieve impressive goals. It comes in all different shapes and sizes. Whether you have an advanced degree or not is a moot point. Always Be Engaged in Learning (ABEL).

Find and enjoy classes in new and different topics. Learn by participating in hobbies, reading, or hands-on by doing something yourself. Learning is directly connected to staying mentally active. Staying mentally active is another important key to achieving greater success in your life.

Make a list of learning opportunities for yourself. Include new learning opportunities in your schedule.

- Set a goal to read a book, watch a video, or connect to a podcast about new topics that might help you recognize and pursue profitable new opportunities.

Remember... **"Whether you think you can or think you can't, you're right!"**   Henry Ford

Conclusion

Now that you have been introduced to these ten principles, what will you do with this information? Your success in this life is totally up to you. If you learn something new from this book, but take no action to implement this knowledge into your life, you really have learned nothing at all. You must act... take action... do something new. If you will act upon just one new idea today, it can change the trajectory of your entire life! You are the captain of your life.

Consider that an experienced captain of an airplane can fly from New York City to Paris, France with ease. However, if the plane should get off course just one or two degrees during the trip, the airplane will end up in an entirely different country hundreds of miles away from the desired destination. The brain is a super computer. As you program it for life's journey, it will not fail. Your super computer will keep you on the beam and steadily moving forward in your life. Use your tool kit to help chart your successful journey to prosperity, happiness, wealth, and greater achievements beyond. Best wishes on your exciting journey.

www.ingramcontent.com/pod-product-compliance
Lightning Source LLC
LaVergne TN
LVHW010220070526
838199LV00062B/4667